Don't Borrow

$ Money $

Until ...

You Read This Book!

Don't Borrow
$ Money $
Until ...
You Read This Book!

Paul E. Counter

White Knight Publications
Toronto Ontario Canada

Author contact: dontborrowmoney@sympatico.ca

Published in 2003 by White Knight Publications,
a division of Bill Belfontaine Limited.
Suite 103, One Benvenuto Place
Toronto Ontario Canada M4V 2L1
T. 416-925-6458   F. 416-925-4165
E-mail whitekn@istar.ca

Ordering information
Hushion House
c/o Georgetown Terminal Warehouses
34 Armstrong Avenue, Georgetown ON, L7G 4R9
Tel: 866-485-5556   Fax: 866-485-6665
e-mail: bsisnett@gtwcanada.com

National Library of Canada Cataloguing in Publication

Counter, P.E. (Paul Ernst), 1968-
Don't borrow money until you read this book / P.E. Counter.
ISBN 0-9730949-6-6
1. Loans, Personal. I. Title.

HG3755.C68 2003   332.7'43   C2003-901584-X

Cover and Text Design: Karen Petherick,
                                Intuitive Design International Ltd.
Art Treatment: Janson
Editing: Bill Belfontaine
Printed and Bound in Canada

DEDICATION

I dedicate this project to my wife Tracy, and children Kathryn and Joshua whose love, support, and encouragement throughout were most sincerely needed and appreciated. On the early mornings and late nights while the light stilled burned and the children slept, nothing could be heard but a scribbling pen or ticking keyboard. The smell of fresh coffee brewing kept me going more times than not!

Thanks for manning the fort Tracy while I was engrossed.

To those readers who will become more knowledgeable borrowers I hope the information provided helps them achieve a better end now that the secret to borrowing is in their hands.

ACKNOWLEDGEMENTS

I am pleased to acknowledge the assistance provided by the following people, without whom this book may not have been published.

To Karen Petherick of Intuitive Design International Ltd., for her talented rendition of a dynamic, eye-catching cover and easily-read interior design,

To Bill Belfontaine who edited my manuscript and made many concrete suggestions that inspired creative additions that will benefit the reader and borrower,

To White Knight Publications who believed in my desire to help people depending on financial institutions to borrow money,

To Darlene Montgomery who lead the publicity campaign for this project. Thanks for your dedication Darlene, and for helping to get this title the media exposure it was looking for,

To TransUnion Credit Bureau who were open to discussion about their service,

And finally, to all those who so influenced my life that I could arrive at this point in my banking career where I have acquired the knowledge to perceive the need for this book and to write it in such a way as it can become a valuable asset to persons of all ages.

I thank them all, most sincerely.

Paul Counter

TABLE OF CONTENTS

Foreword

PART ONE
Organizing Your Affairs

FOREWORD

In many years of dealing with clients, a common trend emerged over most others: People, in general, do not have a grasp of what exactly a bank looks for when they walk through the bank's entrance to ask to borrow money.

It's almost predictable that the average person will share their story, then leave it in the lenders' hands to interpret, perceive (or forget) what they had just heard. Sometimes, just a small point in their story will skid them the wrong way before they really started on their loan application. After all, how can a lender forget something they just heard and still be responsible to their employer?

I've lost track of the number of times that I thought that a book should be available for people to acquire that would help them properly understand and navigate through the modern lending process. A book that would put customers back in the driver seat when they visited one of the most needed and least understood companies in the world, a bank.

Benefits shared by me were received from enquiry, reading, observations, researching, and by delving into my personal life and professional experiences that added to my ability to provide concise information, in the effort to do just this;

Assist people to find the best position for their financial affairs so they will increase their opportunities to achieve an approved loan application, and of most importance, to properly manage their credit file.

If you lock away in your mind the tips presented throughout this book they will help you build your strategies to achieve and maintain good financial health.

When I talk about banks, please keep in mind I am referring to financial institutions in general (trust companies, credit unions, etc.). I am not referring to any one bank or financial institution over another for the process, approach or products they offer. I do not imply to know everything there is to know about each financial institution in Canada and the USA but the information I provide is a great base line to enhance your efforts to be more fruitful. The processes and guidelines of each financial institution will vary. However, their fundamental need to review loan applications remains common, and this book provides a customer's map for this need.

Pay special attention to the personal security and identity theft sections for their added value information to help protect you and family from serious loss and embarrassment.

Think about the questions raised throughout each section. If you identify an area of personal concern that requires changing your way of doing things, then think through what you want to accomplish, make the change, and move on. At the end of the day only you can initiate that change in your own financial affairs, nobody else.

PART ONE

Organizing Your Affairs

CHAPTER 1

If They'd Only Known!

THIS BOOK WAS WRITTEN TO HELP THE AVERAGE PERSON understand, especially those just starting out at university or their careers, what exactly they would be getting into when approaching a lending institution for a loan. I remember walking into a bank for the first time to seek a loan. Not only was I poorly prepared I had no idea how the system worked and I was destined to fail before I began because I didn't know there was a starting line or where it was located. If I'd only known the information presented in these pages I would have had a fighting chance to win the first time out!

We'll talk about how to better position your applications when you apply, minimizing your trial-and-error with a bank and maximize your confidence so you get a better deal. You will also understand how to prepare for your *client interview* with a loan officer, what to say and what <u>not</u> to say, and how to establish and maintain a good credit profile. We'll look at paying bills on time and managing credit cards appropriately so they don't manage you. Most importantly you'll learn how to obtain, read, and manage your credit bureau report so that it becomes the best *financial fingerprint* to describe your life.

I'll be your guide using my extensive financial experience and insider knowledge during this safari through the jungle of modern lending. I want to help you to use your credit bureau reports to become your protective shield and not a weapon of destruction decided by an electronic program that handles your credit application.

I will tell you, quite frankly, what it felt like for one young family I know when they found themselves hostage to a bank-lending paradox. It is a typical first-time experience where many people find themselves being tripped up while taking their first steps. It is a true example, and when you relate to the next few pages, you will enjoy the rest of this book!

— • —

Nicholas tried turning the ignition key again, but it was no use, not even a click. In his heart he reasoned (hoped, actually) that if he tried it enough times the car would suddenly start as if it had been playing a big joke on him.

But no, it had finally expired as it had not made it through the night. He needed to be at work in 40 minutes and had a twenty-minute drive to get there. His bank account was overdrawn, and he had no idea how he was going to affect the badly needed repair. Payday, sadly, was also a week away.

It was early morning mid-February, and bitterly cold. The kind of cold that whispers as it settles its way deep in your bones, *"You better hurry ... I've come to freeze you!"* His fog-like breath frosted out the view through the windshield. The car keys swung slowly to a stop in the ignition and it became ominously quiet in the darkness of early morning.

Nicholas yanked the keys from the ignition, scooped up his things, and went back inside. Megan had just finished changing their new baby, Katie, and had put her down for a morning sleep. It could have been the look on his face or the many times that she had seen it before, she knew the car hadn't started.

Instead of seething in anger, they thought about it differently. They realized that using the amount they were spending on repairs could likely afford a small bank loan for something newer.

Nicholas called his employer and explained his situation, again. He could tell by the sound in his voice that if it happened many more times he would lose his job. They shared a morning coffee while working on a budget; sure they could repay a small bank loan back over three years. When Katie woke from her morning sleep they bundled her up and made their way to the closest branch of their bank. He didn't think his employer would allow him any more time away from work, so their problem had to be solved today!

Nicholas opened the door for Megan pushing Katie in her stroller. He couldn't remember the last time he'd gone into a branch of his bank, other than to use the automated teller machine (ATM). It was the first time he had actually spent to take a good look around.

A general buzz of business activity took place in front of each teller that signalled impatience to serving the unending line of clients. Nicholas read a large 'Mutual Fund' sign hung from the ceiling at least ten times, before they got to the wicket to be served. More than ten customers were shuffling forward whenever the next available teller was available. It seemed for every person that left the line another would join in on the end, making the line-up endless.

As he unzipped his coat he wondered what was a mutual fund?

It was their turn to step forward in the line-up to be served next. The teller in front of them broke the news that they were waiting in the wrong line, and should go to the front desk for assistance with arranging an appointment with a lender.

With his heart doing flip-flops, they found their way to the front desk. He had never asked a bank for money before, and wasn't sure how to start. Nicholas looked around and it didn't help to see that most people were dressed professionally. He had already changed at home into his best clothes, though he still seemed casual in the midst of all these people. His tie was a hand-me-down from somewhere, and if it were a sheet of paper it would have yellowed from age. He wore winter boots with the cuffs of his slacks tucked into them to stay dry. Feeling more and more out of place, he fought back the anxiety to just turn and leave. Katie began to fuss from being too hot inside from the cold, and Megan starting peeling off winter layers.

Nicholas asked the person at the front desk who they needed to speak with for a small bank loan. "Natalie" was pinned neatly to her lapel.

"What is the first letter of your last name please?" she asked a little impatiently, which didn't help the way he felt.

"R," he replied, wondering if she was going to ask

him his first name, or for that matter the remaining letters to spell the rest of his last name. He smiled to Megan sitting with Katie in the waiting area and she smiled back. Katie squeaked and babbled baby talk oblivious to everything, especially her tensed-up father.

"Your account manager is Beatrice. She handles all clients whose last name starts with R. I'll ask if she is available to see you."

Nicholas joined Megan in the waiting area, and explained the name of their account manager. It sounded odd. They never knew they had an account manager to talk to them before. Nicholas followed Natalie with his eyes toward Beatrice's cubicle until she disappeared inside. He wondered what was said as she quickly returned to where they were sitting with the same busy hustle that fuelled the entire branch.

Natalie said Beatrice was booked solid all day and would not be able to see them. She also explained they should have called in advance to make an appointment. To avoid this from happening again they were handed their account manager's card, then told to have a nice day.

Before Natalie could turn and leave Nicholas jumped up saying, "I need to speak with someone today as I can't take another day off work." Though he didn't want to sound as if he were pleading, he knew he was, "Are you sure no one else can see us?"

Natalie looked at the various account managers' diaries and said all were booked for the day with appointments. She thought again about Beatrice, as she should make time to see them before anyone else.

Natalie returned from their account manager's office with the good news that Beatrice would squeeze them in between her next appointment.

Gathering their things they followed toward Beatrice's cubical like lemmings. They had no idea what to say or expect as they were at the mercy of their account manager's perception to understand their needs and take care of the problem they had.

They exchanged pleasantries while Beatrice appeared to forgive them for disrupting her schedule.

Megan explained that they had worked on their budget, and they had determined they could afford to repay a $3,000 loan over three years. Nicholas described the overwhelming need for a reliable vehicle to be able to go to work and school. It was clear that without his current employment there would be no money to repay anything, and they very much relied on a vehicle to make their plan work.

Beatrice listened attentively as they spoke, not once interrupting. Actually, in the silence the couple felt they needed to explain more. That perhaps Beatrice needed to hear something special in their sincerity, for her to grant them the loan. After they had shared all they could to better present why they needed the loan, how desperately they needed a reliable vehicle; their account manager took control of the meeting, "How long have you been working at your current job?"

"I've been at this job for six months, and also have a part time job as a waiter. I've been a waiter for over a year." Hearing himself describe his employment history was difficult, it sounded weak, but he had always brought home a pay cheque, and that had to count for something in their favour. Megan looked after other children throughout the day, and between the two of them they managed to pay all their bills on time.

"Nicholas, can you please sign this form for me? It allows me to pull a credit bureau to review your repayment history."

He signed, not understanding what 'pull' meant, or what a credit bureau was. After all, this was a bank and if anyone were going to watch over him, it would be them.

Beatrice began typing on her keyboard. Within moments she stopped, turned and drew a breath, "Aside from one item on your credit bureau, you have no credit history."

"What does that mean?" he asked while questions started buzzing in his head. What did this have to do with his need for $3,000? What else does she need to know? He felt they had clearly explained why they needed the loan and that they could repay it.

"It means that you have no debt that we can review to prove you meet your commitments. It also means that the one item that is not good on your report is also holding you back from obtaining new credit."

Nicholas was confused. Megan's look almost said out loud, "What?".

Recovering his thoughts he asked, "We have never missed a cable or phone bill payment, and have always paid our rent on time. What do you mean we don't have a credit history?"

"That doesn't count Nicholas, everyone has to pay these bills or those companies would cut their service. You need to have a loan or credit card to establish credit," she stated.

"That's why we're here."

Avoiding the paradox, she went on to say, "You also have to deal with the derogatory item on your credit bureau."

"What is it?" he asked.

"I can't tell you, you need to request your own credit bureau report to see it yourself."

"Isn't it right there in front of you?"

"Yes, but it belongs to the bank and I'm not at liberty to show you."

"It's my report. I allowed you to look at it. Why can't you show me?"

"I'm not allowed to show you," was the final answer.

(It turned out that later Nicholas learned it was someone else's information mixed up on his credit report in error, but it didn't help his situation any now.)

"You also have a high TDS ratio Nicholas. Unfortunately we will not be able to offer you a loan today." Yet she proceeded to encourage him, "Try coming back in about six months when you clean your credit report up and have been at your full-time job for over a year."

The meeting was over before they knew it. Katie happily hadn't begun to fuss from sitting so long and that was the only happiness they had going at that moment. Megan and Nicholas stared at each other, wondering if there was more that could be done. The look on Beatrice's face said there wasn't and she appeared to become impatient to begin her next appointment.

They surfed through acceptance of their situation, grasping at anything to keep the interview going. "What does TDS mean?" he asked, trying to comprehend why they were being declined.

"Here's a brochure that explains TDS and GDS. It will help you to understand what we look for when reviewing loan applications."

He took the brochure and stuffed it slowly into his

pocket. "How can I get to see a copy of my credit report?" He had never seen it, and honestly had no idea such a report was available on him. It seemed very cloak-and-dagger like they knew more about him than he did.

"Try calling this number," she said as she jotted on a yellow sticky note, "and they'll describe how you can obtain and read your credit bureau report."

That was it. They were declined before they made it past the first five minutes. She never asked Megan a question.

As if on autopilot, they found themselves outside the branch standing in the parking lot while snow quietly fell around them, blinded by the blizzard of confusion that modern technology had heaped on them. They were caught in a log jam of procedure that they didn't know existed until they pushed a stroller through the bank's doorway. Nicholas wondered what had just happened, and more importantly, what could they do to get out of their dilemma.

— • —

If this short account of another borrower's problem sounds at all familiar to you, or happened to someone you know, then don't stop reading this book! You can, by the time you reach the last page, be able to walk into a bank with confidence and the understanding that you have taken the appropriate steps to position yourself for a loan.

That day had Nicholas and Megan understood the impact of a credit bureau report, or if they had known how to position their financial affairs properly, the application process would have taken a different turn.

That same five minute interview could have ended differently; they could have bought that newer car a few days later and been able to follow through with their plans.

Do you wonder where they are today? Probably in a lifestyle that means a lot to them, as we hope they were able to receive that job-saving loan from somewhere.

CHAPTER 2

Myths On Borrowing

Paying your bills on time

Commonly, people assume because they pay their bills regularly their credit is strong. This is not entirely true. Simply paying your bills irrespective of the due date isn't always as important as *when* you pay your bills.

Have you ever found yourself between paydays, and your credit card payment is due? Did you know waiting those few days to your next salary cheque before paying actually has an impact on your credit rating? Your card payment, after the 30 day due date is now classified as "30 days late" and is reported to the credit bureau by your card provider. Had you made a partial payment of even 10 dollars, you wouldn't be late, short paid, perhaps, but not late. Only non-payments (not partial payments) are reported and affect your credit rating. So this means that even if you're between paydays and short of cash, pay *something* toward your bills and keep that precious credit rating clean!

Credit cards

How many credit cards do you need?

Imagine that you just walked into your favourite department store, and in your path sits a sales representative behind a small folding table. In front of them are pads of blank application forms attached to clipboards, with a pen dangling from a length of string.

The pitch begins, "Would you like to apply for our credit card? It takes only a few minutes of your time."

As you consider the time you'd spend (which you never seem to have enough of) the representative adds value by offering a free gift hoping you'll apply just to get the gift. Your eyes light up as you spot that pen set you've been longing for! Without a second thought you pick up the clipboard and begin enthusiastically to complete the application. The sales representative behind the table smiles, assures you that you'll receive a letter in the mail advising of your approval (or decline) in a week or so, and then you're on your way. Ten minutes maximum. Makes you feel good to know you'll have "the" card in case you need it.

Store staff try to interest as many people as possible to complete an application. They are paid a bonus in some cases on how many completed applications they can collect during their stint at the table. They don't care if you qualify or not! All they care about is convincing you this department store's credit card is perfect for your needs. (They don't tell you their interest rates are 10-20% more than a regular line of credit would be with your bank!).

So what happens with your application? Why are they trying to collect such a large volume of new applications?

Good question!

Once the representative folds the table, your application is delivered by courier to a central processing centre, where it is keyed into a computer, then reviewed by a sophisticated computer software program that spits out a decline or approval based on how well your application *scored*. A letter is then automatically printed and mailed informing you of their decision. The more applications the computer-scoring model reviews, the more volume of approved credit cards the department store is able to issue. More cards mean more people carrying a balance and paying interest and that is a very healthy increase for the merchant and loan company.

They not only want your borrowing power (that also increases theirs), they also want their plastic in your wallet. Once in your wallet you're more likely to shop at their store over another. This is referred to as securing wallet share, or trying to keep a piece of your wallet (spending) while at the same time keeping their competitors away from you.

Just to keep things in proper perspective, lets review the answers to a few questions you should ask.

Does this credit card company have your best interests in mind or their own?

While you're completing their clipboard application you're making many choices, most of which you're likely to be unaware:

You decided that it was okay for this department store to look at your credit rating, and see all the credit you have including credit with their competitors. They can see what credit limits are available to you and what your present balances are. They can see your repayment history for every credit card, loan, or car payment you ever made!

They know if someone has placed a collection item against you, and if you have not paid a debt in the past.

You were also asked to complete an address section, which updates your credit bureau to establish your current address. If you have moved recently, anybody reviewing your credit background will see first how transient you are. Had you not applied, no one would have known.

You likely identified whether you're single, married or common-law. This will be updated on your bureau report and may seem harmless. Keep in mind the Canadian Human Rights Act (CHRA) states banks cannot ask for spousal information if the spouse is not a joint applicant, unless relying on alimony, child support or separation payments from them. You may find that applying completely on your own has a greater impact on whether you're approved. After all, is it anybody's business what your marital status is when you're paying all your bills from your own income?

There will come a time when you apply and your spouse's credit bureau report will also be reviewed. The benefit of two incomes also carries with it the prior repayment history of each applicant. Challenge your individual rights to privacy based on marital status, sexual orientation, religion, and other personal information! Question how anyone knowing this helps determine the risk in being repaid. It would be interesting to see what they would say in response! Having said that, don't offer additional information unless you determine it's necessary. When you advise you have a spouse, you also present the risk that you have dependents (though in today's world this should be a poor conclusion). Children are a risk only so far as they represent an additional commitment for cash each month while you meet the increasing needs of your family. Plainly put, you're likely to feed them before paying your bills. Also, if you identify you have two children, then complete another application later on and advise you have only one child the question is now begged, *"Do you have to pay child support?"*

You have revealed how long you've worked for your present employer, your salary, and your position with your company. This information can be compared against the last time you applied for credit and entered similar details. Someone reviewing your bureau report can identify how transient your employment is, and when completing a future application are able to determine your employment tendencies. How long do you stay at one job? Are you unemployed regularly in the same industry? Did your employment or salary change from the last time you applied for credit?

There are many things kept on a database for all to see and use. Each time you apply for credit you're also giving written consent for someone to review your credit bureau report. You're also updating that information in more detail each time you apply for credit. The more information on a person's credit bureau report, the more complete a lender's perception becomes, and scoring models (which we'll review later on) become more refined.

Well, look at the bright side; after completing the in-store credit application you did get a free pen set!

How do too many credit cards work against you?

Did you know that the more credit cards you have, the less borrowing power you have readily available?

Its great when you may belong to the population of people that can actually pay their credit cards to zero each month (55% of all borrowers), but all that shows is that you're adverse to debt. Don't misunderstand, nominal debt does minimize the risk in lending to you but each card you carry has its own limit. Even though you pay your cards to zero each month you have the choice to max them all. With this in mind banks calculate about 2-5% of the limit that needs to be paid. This reduces the amount of cash you have each month to service debt on paper, even though you pay your cards monthly. Sounds silly I know, but you do have the option to maximize the amount of debt on your cards at any time and your bank will take that into consideration when lending to you.

How many different credit cards do you need?

Try getting a low interest charge card from your bank, or a line of credit linked to your account for point of sale purchases. Cut up all your other credit cards and cancel their use in writing and keep a dated copy. This decision carries with it a few other benefits other than simply one card to worry about. Your bank now respects your decision to carry their card, and that adds value to your relationship when looking for additional credit at that bank. If you also have other bank credit cards it's considered you share your banking relationships, and no bank likes to share your wallet with another.

Sharing your banking relationships can become a yellow flag in the lending process as bankers see a risk for "kiting" (floating money between accounts to cover the same group of cheques, where a fraudulent person has the ability to access cash that isn't theirs—until caught!). Banks have very sophisticated systems in place that do nothing but track deposit behaviours of people and cross check those behaviours against fraudulent profiles. Kiting is illegal, and subject to prosecution.

Shared banking relationships are viewed cautiously, where a single banking relationship adds strength to your application. Decide on a single credit card and perhaps one department store's credit card to meet your needs. Limits usually can be adjusted as well, depending on your needs, with a quick call in most cases.

How high should your credit limit be?

What if you have only a few credit cards with high limits you never use? This is not to your benefit. Request them to be reduced to a level that meets your needs. Each time you receive a letter or phone call advising you of your valued business, and your new limit, they have decreased your borrowing power in the hopes you will maximize your potential to use their card. If you don't need or use your maximum credit limit, reduce it to a level that's right for you. Don't let the card company arbitrarily increase your limits without first asking you, tying up your borrowing power on their share of your wallet.

Why do card companies keep raising my limit when I don't ask?

The card companies increase your limits arbitrarily without calling you for a number of reasons. You may have been identified as paying the credit card down regularly, and have proven to be of nominal risk. Keep in mind it's not an official increase unless you chose to use it. It is only an *approved* increase. This is why only the maximum amount of each card is reflected on the credit bureau report. Just because it's approved for your usage, doesn't mean you have accepted the liability. Using the increase is acceptance to the approval. If you don't want it, don't use it. Better still, call the card company and ask them to reduce the limit to what it was before so you're not tempted to use it impulsively.

Some credit cards have points that you collect while others offer discounts; but all want you to carry a balance so they can earn interest revenue from you (18% a year is not unusual). They also earn revenue from the businesses that accept your credit card as payment each time it is used whether you carry a balance or not. The business is charged a fee per transaction, often based on the dollar amount of your purchase. The larger your purchase, the larger the fee for that transaction charged to the merchant. Raising your limit so often encourages these larger purchases, and create larger balances on your credit card, so be careful how you use your card.

CHAPTER 3

Credit Bureau "Hits"

There is a slang credit bureau report expression known as a "hit," which refers to the action that occurs when a copy of your credit bureau report is requested by computer.

Many believe that no one will know where or how many times they have applied for credit. Just as naively, they also believe that it doesn't matter. Why not apply and see if you'll get that new department store credit card? Who cares? You get a free plastic container or pen set just for completing an application!

Each time you apply for funds, another credit bureau report is pulled into your application electronically. This happens regardless if you apply numerous times at the same bank, or several other banks. Each time your report is pulled, it negatively impacts your credit rating, as each bank that requests your report counts as a hit. If this applies to you—SURPRISE! You've just been identified as a "credit seeker"! It is very easy to see how many times a person has applied for credit, where they have applied, and then assumptions can be made whether you were approved or not, simply by seeing if a new "Trade Line" has been opened on your report.

If you complete a department store in-store credit application for furniture or appliances it also counts as applying for credit and is reported to your credit bureau. The paper application you completed is faxed to a centralized adjudication centre (similar to the department stores application), where the information you provided is keyed into a software-scoring model and reviewed. And as you guessed it by now, I'm sure, this scoring model pulls a copy of your most recent credit bureau report into the application for analysis.

The last thing shown on your report (aside from collection items and bankruptcy information), is information on everyone who's requested your report, including the date they requested it. Preserve the quality of your credit bureau information by minimizing the number of people who could request it. Remember, you're free to request a copy of your file at any time, and it is never reported on your bureau that you received a copy. This assists you in maintaining the quality of the information contained in it. (Please review Chapter 7—Understanding your Credit Bureau.)

When you feel that your application has been reviewed with prejudice, ask for the ombudsman office contact number (which must be provided when asked for), requesting a review. That office reviews the bank's response to a client's needs, and suggests a decision for a course of action after understanding each individual perception involved of the facts, and often after facilitating joint conversations to reach mutual agreements. Usually most misunderstandings are nothing more than that, a misunderstanding. Bringing in a third party to reflect on the file often adds clarity to all parties involved. Major banks today have no tolerance for prejudices or diversity conflicts that determine a credit decision. Their centralized adjudication or credit review facilities are often referred to as a benefit in this regard, as the people reviewing your application only review a compilation of facts and comments, unable to respond to ethnic, religious or diversity issues as these topics are not to be addressed nor commented on. Also, they do not see the client to draw these conclusions themselves though their own personal prejudices may exist.

A list follows of some major Canadian banks that have procedures in place to properly handle customer complaints. I have included their customer service number, ombudsman office contact name and number (as it is at time of writing), along with the financial institution's web site for your convenience.

Contacting your Ombudsman office

CANADIAN BANKING OMBUDSMAN (CBO)
(*canadianbankingombudsman @sympatico.ca*)
Office: 1 888 451-4519
Fax: 1 888 422-2865
www.bankingombudsman.com

BANK OF MONTREAL
Info Service: 1 800 555-3000
Ombudsman: Don Willis (*Small Business Customers Only*)
Office: 1 800 371-2541
Fax: 1 800 766-8029
www.bmo.com

BANK OF NOVA SCOTIA
Customer Service: 1 800 472-6842
Presidents Office: 1 877 700-0043
Ombudsman: Bill Bailey
Office: 1 800 785-8772
Fax (416) 933-3276
www.scotiabank.com

CIBC
Customer info line: 1 800 465-2422
Customer complaint line: 1 800 465-2255
Ombudsman: Milt Maclean
Office: 1 800 308-6859
Fax: 1 800 308-6861
Telecommunications device for the deaf: 1 800 465-7401
www.cibc.com

LAURENTIAN BANK OF CANADA
Customer service: 1 800 522-1846
Ombudsman: Robert Robson
Office: 1 800 473-4782
Fax: 1 800 473-4790
www.laurentianbank.com

NATIONAL BANK OF CANADA
Customer Service: 1 888 835-6281
Ombudsman: Pierre Desroches
Office: 1 888 300-9004
Fax: 1 800 260-80036
www.nbc.ca

ROYAL BANK
Royal Direct: 1 800 769-2599
Customer Relations: 1 800 769-2540
(custrel@royalbank.com)
(ombudsman@royalbank.com)
Office: 1 800 769-2542
Fax: (416) 974-6922
www.rbc.com
www.royalbank.com

TORONTO DOMINION / CANADA TRUST BANK
Customer Service: 1 866 567-8888
Ombudsman: David Fisher
Office: 1 888 361-0319
Fax: (416) 983-3460
www.tdcanadatrust.com

CHAPTER 4

The Difference Between Co-Signers and Co-Borrowers

So your credit application has been declined because of debt servicing. All you need is a co-signer, right? Wrong! Although each case may be reviewed on its own strength, a co-signer by definition is someone who is vouching for you that you can pay or service the debt on your own. It is similar to someone putting in a good word for you but not taking responsibility to assist with the financial commitment each month. A co-signer does not mean that because they have great credit and income that you should be approved on those grounds. You, after all, are the one applying for credit, not the co-signer! Their income is not considered in the application toward servicing your debt, only your income. So if you don't have the cash available monthly to service the new loan you are applying for, you likely won't qualify even with a strong co-signer.

A co-signer adds strength to your application. If in the past you had some mild credit difficulties, i.e., for whatever reason your credit file may show numerous slow payments. A co-signer communicates to the lender that you're past that period and are able to meet your commitments going forward. If you're not, the co-signer will pay for you. Understand now that the bank isn't as much concerned about who pays, as long as they are paid. Your co-signer may be requested to obtain Independent Legal Advise (ILA) before the bank will accept their signature in any legal way to your application.

So, what if the bank isn't comfortable with your application because of more serious issues? Perhaps you started a new job, or have moved around a lot, or simply have no credit or very poor, or very little, credit history. Banks may be willing to review your application further with the strength of a *co-borrower*. A co-borrower agrees with you to share the responsibility of the debt equally. Commonly an account is set up in joint names of all borrowers from where the payment is to be taken. In the event of non-payment, the creditor can request full payment from all borrowers involved (also known as a *joint and several* guarantee). Each borrower and co-borrower's income is taken into consideration to service debt, and adds much more strength to your application than simply a co-signer. This is common for car purchases and mortgages. Banks usually like to ensure they have "a back door" should something turn wrong after the money has been loaned. In this case, the back door would be that full repayment could be demanded from any borrower instead of the Bank chasing down all borrowers for an equal portion of one guarantee.

CHAPTER 5

Debt Servicing

Your monthly budget likely accounts for every dollar coming into your home. Perhaps detailing each payment and expense you'll be required to pay for that month while the amount of cash left over you designate toward savings. When you're sitting at your kitchen table trying to calculate if you can afford another loan, I bet you review that extra cash you're currently putting toward savings to cover your new loan payment. This may reduce the amount left over for savings at the end of each month, but all your bills will be paid. Surely a bank understands this, and will make that new loan to you.

Well, it really isn't that simple as it depends on how much of your cash income goes toward covering Principal and Interest (P&I) payments each month. Canadian Mortgage and Housing Corporation (CMHC Canada) defines *Gross Debt Servicing* (GDS) and *Total Debt Servicing* (TDS) ratios and provides acceptable levels in their pocket reference booklet dated 05/2000:

GDS ratio
The borrower must not commit more than 32% of gross household income toward the payment of

principal + interest + property taxes + heat. (For condominiums, this formula must also include 50% of condominium fees. For chattel loans, it must include site rents.)

TDS ratio

The borrower must not commit more than 40% of gross household income toward housing obligations and all other debts. (Total principal and interest payments + payments on all other debts X 100.)

A copy of the pocket guide, which must be used only as a reference, can be obtained from most banks free. Call CMHC direct at 1-888-463-6454 for further explanation or visit their web page at: www.cmhc.ca.

Self-employed individuals may find it a challenge when borrowing funds as they usually position their lifestyle around their business expenses. This reduces the amount of income they report to Canada Customs and Revenue Agency (CCRA, formerly Revenue Canada) and the tax they are required to pay. Although this is a good way to reduce taxable income, it adversely affects GDS and TDS ratios. In most cases self-employed people need to review their tax returns with the lender when applying for credit. Commonly they are able to add items back into income that were declared expenses such as: depreciation, amortization, capital cost allowances, interest, and one-time expenses to name a few. It is most likely lenders will only add back depreciation, amortization and capital cost allowances when lending to a sole owner using their tax return as evidence of income. If they need to add back many small items in order to prove GDS and TDS your request may be viewed as being too risky and declined.

It is also important to note that most lenders will require you to be in business at least three years before using your self-employed income to service debt. Banks like to review historical information to establish likely trends. By reviewing three years of tax returns they are able to establish the direction in which you're headed and an average income likely to continue through the life of the new loan for which you're now applying.

If you're a self-employed sole owner, consider carefully your tax structure and planning to include the necessary income required for personal and business debt combined. Also consider immediate and future needs to establish a historical ability to service future needs. This room can be found not only in net earnings, but also in draws, depreciation, amortization, and additional forms of receivables.

It is a good idea to have a meeting with your accountant and banker to review your three-year plan. Know now what you want to own or buy, and position your financial affairs to service that debt. Meeting with your accountant and banker helps add clarity to what everybody needs to do to help you reach your goals. (Please review Chapter 10—Your Income And How You Report It, for more sole proprietor information.)

Equity lending

Even though you may only be requesting to borrow 50% of the value of an asset you intend to purchase, that doesn't mean a bank will automatically finance the balance for you. Lending in this respect is referred to as *Equity Lending* (EL), or lending against the value of an asset.

Financing such as EL reflects a strategy that if you don't meet your commitments the lender will own the asset, then selling it to recover the money owed by the borrower. This ensures that you have money invested in the asset as well, and likely don't want to lose the equity you've built up and will be more willing to pay as agreed.

EL is commonly seen when financing mortgages, or lending to a business. At the end of the day, despite how small your loan may be compared to the value of the asset, cash is the only thing that repays debt. If you can't prove you have the necessary amount of cash to meet regular monthly payments you won't get your loan or mortgage approved. Even if all you need is $5,000 financing on a $1,000,000 asset!

CHAPTER 6

Establishing Credit

What if you've never had credit in your name before?

Finding credit needs to be approached as if you're trying to find a really good job. Anybody can shotgun a dozen resumes around hoping someone calls them. Fewer research the type of job they prefer doing and whom they prefer doing it with. These few are better prepared to land the job they want, where they want. Finding credit for the first time is similar to finding a really good job. It needs to be done smartly, and you need to be prepared.

 On occasion, it is very sensible to borrow in advance of a need. This starts to establish a strong credit history because you will pay it back promptly or could provide the needed cash prior to a financial concern.

Four easy steps ...
   to help you become prepared

1. **Complete your Personal Statement of Affairs (PSOA)**

a) This is a snapshot picture of what you owe compared to what you own. If you don't have credit this will be a simple list to make. When you have credit, be sure to list all your bank loans, credit cards and car payments beside the assets they helped finance.

b) If, after making this list, you find that the amount of debt is greater than the value of the assets you own, you have "a negative net worth." If this is true for you, it will grow increasingly difficult to obtain new debt without the value of an asset linked to it to maintain the balance. For example; a loan for a motorcycle may be easier to obtain than an unsecured line of credit, or additional hard security may be required (cash, investments, or collateral mortgage on your property will need to be taken).

c) On the same piece of paper include your monthly living expenses and all forms of income to determine whether you can afford new debt before applying for it. At the end of the day it doesn't matter if a bank grants you a new loan or not if you can't pay it back! Be sure you can pay before applying. If you've decided you're not likely to get the loan you want to apply for, *then don't apply*! Make an appointment with a bank to review your situation. They will either confirm of deny your feelings without requesting a copy of your credit bureau report.

d) Banks usually provide options and actions you can take to better position yourself for the next time you apply. Write down their advice, read it back to them to establish a commitment from them that if you followed their direction, they would quite likely be interested in lending to you later. When in agreement, this list becomes a checklist for you on what the bank needs to see in order to lend to you.

e) Take time on this step to determine how you will present yourself and sell your strengths (savings, assets, stable employment and address for more than a year or two) in this snapshot.

 You will find the templates in Chapters 11 and 12 helpful when completing your Personal Statement of Affairs.

2. Review your budget

a) Once your PSOA has been completed, review your monthly budget against it to ensure you're able to meet the commitments you already have before taking on a new one. If you can't afford a new loan payment, rethink your options before going to a bank.

3. Review your personal credit bureau report

a) It is important to review your credit rating before you apply for any credit. Call the credit bureaus for a free copy of your report (numbers are listed in *How Your Credit File is Rated* section). If you're not sure how to read it, call them for assistance. Try to completely understand the very document you're attempting to build for your life needs. Today all you may need is a $5,000 loan, but if you're not focused on building strength to your credit rating what about later? What about your first car, or home?

b) If there is derogatory information on your credit file that isn't yours, call the credit bureau and ask how to remove it. Get a letter from the company that reported the item stating it was reported in error. You will need this letter as an attachment when submitting your credit application.

 You will find Chapter 7, Understanding Your Credit Bureau, helpful with more detailed advice on how to manage your credit report.

4. Prove your income

a) You will need to prove your income in any application for credit. Banks will ask for proof in the form of a recent employment T4 slip, recent notice of assessment and possibly a copy of your last tax return. A notice of assessment arrives from CCRA, six to eight weeks after they have reviewed your personal tax return. You may also be asked for a recent pay stub or employment letter.

b) I recommend having all of these available for your client interview.

100% Cash secured credit cards

At one time people were able to walk into a bank with $1,000 cash to secure their first $1,000 credit card. Their new card was 100% cash secured which removed most risk from the bank to help someone establish themselves. Seems simple enough. Today however, times have changed. For many reasons this is no longer widely accepted, and I would be surprised if a major Canadian bank still offered this type of product.

Student credit cards are sometimes easier to get, as it is understood this age group is attempting to establish their credit. If you are a student I recommend you apply for this type of credit to help establish your credit history early on. If you are not a student, unfortunately you won't qualify.

For most it is easier to obtain credit from a department store, or retail outlet your first time verses applying with your bank. Buying a piece of furniture from one of the stores that doesn't need to be paid for a year is a good way to establish some credit. Though this type of buying can be expensive, it is an easier credit than most to obtain.

Financing for these promotions often are at higher interest rates than banks and carry penalty charges should you not meet your commitments. You are in effect establishing a good reference by using this type of financing so the next time someone looks at your credit file they will see your furniture debt paid in full.

Your phone, cable, and general utility bills will likely not appear on your credit bureau. The only time (presently) these trade lines will appear on your report is when you don't pay them and they go to collection. They currently are not members of the bureaus and therefore don't publicly report your account information. This tells us unfortunately, that even though you may be meeting your commitments with these services, there's no weight attached to your credit bureau because of it. To your benefit, it also does not reveal if you pay them slowly (take 30 or more days to pay your bills).

You will need to obtain some other form of credit to actually have it reported on your credit bureau. Telling a lender that you have an excellent repayment history with the phone, cable or utility provider means nothing. It is expected or you would not have the privilege of these services (the supplier would have cut your service if not paid).

A gas or major department store credit card is also easier than most others to obtain due to their low starting limits of about $500. (Banks don't usually provide credit cards with limits lower than $1,000). You'll find you're trading off a larger interest rate for the privilege of receiving a credit card to help establish yourself. Once your credit is established (at least one to two years) it's a good idea to close the department store and gas cards after replacing them with a conventional bank lower interest credit card (i.e., Visa, MasterCard, or American Express to name a few), it's your decision.

CHAPTER 7

Understanding
Your Credit Bureau

Your credit rating is likely the single most influential factor in the lending process over which you actually have a large degree of control. It is the cumulative result of your borrowing decisions and past history of debt repayment, reflecting the degree of responsibility you have placed on your commitments. A credit file is a portrait of a consumer's financial history with virtually every blemish exposed. Your credit rating is yours and yours alone, and must be guarded as the valuable commodity that it is.

Credit nowadays is a necessity, carrying with it the shadow of your past behaviour. It is a necessary tool when trying to get a cell phone activated, new loan advanced, or credit cards increased and should be monitored closely.

Identity theft

Now is a good time to discuss a growing widespread fraud that is affecting many individuals' personal security and destroying their credit reputation. Be aware that it could impact your life and your credit one day, and guard against it. It's called "identity theft."

This type of fraud involves someone changing your mailing address to receive the credit card applications you normally receive in the mail. Once they have these mailings, they are able (over time and following specific steps) to pretend they are you. With a credit card in their hands with your name on it, they can do many things including destroying your credit rating in the process. If any statements stop arriving in your mail look into it right away! Some people have experienced this type of identity theft so harshly that they have had to change their names to start a new credit history. Do not become naive about crooked people out there who chose to earn a living stealing other people's identity. They are using their stolen credit rating for the purpose of maximizing the borrowing to the hilt, and then leaving the real person to deal with the problem (or bankruptcy).

 Be very aware that you must closely inspect every line of all your monthly statements and that they arrive on time each month, or be suspicious.

I recently learned of an unfortunate experience an individual had when they lost (or had stolen) their wallet. This US attorney experienced first hand how swift identity thieves actually are able to infiltrate personal information, obtain credit, and assume his identity. Within a week, the thieves ordered an expensive monthly cell phone package, applied for a Visa credit card, had a credit line approved to purchase a Gateway computer, received a PIN number from the Department of Motor Vehicles (DMV) to change his driving record information online, and much more.

Protective measures against identity theft

Here are some protective measures you can take to help secure your personal identity and information from these types of ruthless criminals.

- ✔ The next time you order cheques have only your initials, not your first and middle name, put on them. If someone steals your cheque-book they will not know if you sign your cheques with just your initials or your first name, but your bank will. Put your work phone number on your cheques (not your home phone number) to further secure your personal life from someone using a reverse phone directory (a phone book which is organized by phone numbers, not last names) to learn your address. If you have a Post Office box number, use it instead of your home address. Never have your Social Insurance Number (SIN) printed on your cheques.

- ✔ Photo copy all the contents of your wallet, and keep this record in a safe place. If your wallet is ever stolen you will know exactly what was in it, including all your card and account numbers. Include also a photocopy of your passport to this file for when you travel. Keep this file in a very safe place in your home, or safety deposit box at your bank.

✔ Keep a list of all the phone numbers needed to call each card company in the event you need to call them to cancel their card. It is a common error that most people know this, but rarely do this, then find themselves fumbling through phone books and 1-800 numbers to cancel cards where they also have not kept a record of card numbers. The sooner you cancel your cards the less time these thieves have to drill into your personal affairs. Request your replacement card be sent to your bank branch for your pick-up. Don't have them mailed.

✔ If you experience missing statements in your mail, visit the post office outlet that services your community to ensure your address has not been forward to somewhere else without your knowledge. If it has been, notify the authorities immediately.

✔ Try cancelling your credit cards once a year and have a replacement card issued to you. This will prevent old credit card information from being used by thieves, or protect you from a thief who already has your card information but hasn't used it yet.

✔ File a police report immediately in the community where your wallet was lost or stolen. This proves to credit providers you were diligent and is the first step toward an investigation should one be launched.

✔ Call both National Credit Bureaus of Canada (TransUnion and Equifax) to have a fraud alert placed on your credit bureau report. The alert means any company checking your credit bureau report knows your information was stolen and they have to contact you personally to authorize any new credit. This prevents an identity thief from completing on-line credit applications in your name, as the adjudicator reviewing the application would review your credit report as part of their process and observe the alert. This step alone could save your identity, and stop the thieves in their tracks!

✔ Change your PIN or passwords regularly. Try to stay away from using numbers that a thief could easily try that they found in your wallet, i.e., your social insurance number, or birth date. If possible, incorporate combinations of letters and numbers into your passwords, especially for Internet banking. Identity thieves have also been known to transfer entire bank balances to other accounts, withdraw the cash, and then close the account to avoid detection. Don't keep a copy of your PIN or passwords in your wallet or purse.

✔ Buy a personal office paper shredder. They're not expensive and in my opinion are necessary personal devices! Any document that contains personal information should be shredded before you throw it in the trash. This includes utility bills, bank statements, and other invoices you don't retain in your files. Identity thieves are not below stealing your trash if you put it out the night before. They may even steal it in broad daylight. Don't make their job easy!

What does "trade line" mean?

Every credit card, loan, line of credit or lease you have ever had is recorded on a *trade line* of your credit bureau report. Each trade line has a repayment summary which calculates the number of times your payments were late (30, 60 and 90 days), the amount of the authorized limit (or your credit limit on your cards), their balances and monthly minimum payments as well as an overall credit rating for that lending product. It also reveals if bankruptcy was ever filed for, and so on.

From this report lenders are able to verify the loans you tell them about that are with other banks.

As mentioned earlier there are also items that don't show up on your credit bureau that you might think should be there such as cable and telephone companies. These companies do however, keep records, so be cautious before withholding payment! If you are disputing a charge or refuse to pay, the amount may appear as a collection item on your credit file, which is seen by all that pull a copy of your report.

Most banks don't report overdraft credit facility on your regular chequing and savings accounts either. So even though you have access to an overdraft, lenders most often can't confirm this from your report alone. You need to tell them the name of each bank where you have an overdraft.

Keep in mind you will be asked to answer a question relating to other loans or additional credit not reported in an effort to gain full disclosure from you about your financial affairs. It is looked upon with favour when everything is disclosed. If they discover you withheld an important detail purposely, they begin to lose confidence in you as a client (perhaps flag you for possibly commit-ting fraud) and the application process becomes more difficult as you go along now and in the future with this bank.

FYI: Mortgages and your credit bureau report

You may be surprised to learn most banks don't report your mortgage balance or repayment history to a credit bureau agency! When you review your own report your mortgage will not appear on it. There's no mistake. This also means, similar to overdrafts and private loans, a lender reviewing your application for credit has no way of knowing unless you tell them that you have a mortgage that's using up cash each month from your income by reviewing only your credit report. There are ways they can find out if you have a mortgage, though it is commonly not done nowadays. Lenders usually don't have the time available to verify such things. It is commonplace for them to take a client's word when they say they own their home free-and-clear, if they are also able to explain how they did it (i.e., their parents gave them an earlier inheritance; it was a wedding gift; the house was passed down to them through an inheritance from a grandparent; perhaps they did very well on the stock market, etc.).

It is prudent to tell the truth early on, to establish trust in your relationship with banks. Revealing all unknowns upfront provides continual comfort going forward for financial institutions, referred to as "knowing" their client. Micro details, later on at times, can be overlooked when they "know" you. (There is a disadvantage to revealing all, which we will discuss in Chapter 16.)

When offering your home as collateral security there is a title search performed. If you have lied about not having a mortgage it will be discovered and your relationship with the bank compromised. You likely will be asked to find another bank for *all* your needs. When trust has been compromised, they likely will not do business with you again.

They are not allowed to share what they know about you to other banks, or lending institutions. Your file is confidential to them, as they report your repayment history to the credit bureaus only. This means if you have a poor relationship with one bank, they are not allowed to share this information with others to warn them. This also provides a second chance for you to start fresh with a new bank if you've had problems with the one you're with now.

I do not recommend anyone lie, or distort the facts. That doesn't do anybody any good. I share these uncommon facts to illustrate that while most banks rely heavily on the information your credit report file contains about you, sometimes it works against them through it's incompleteness as much as it works against you when the information on your file is false. Though credit report information is weak at times, they are still the only regulated source of financial repayment history the modern banking system has to rely on that is arbitrarily collected from various sources.

The credit bureau was not designed to be a summary of all your loans, credit cards or bank accounts. It was designed to simply act as a reference for would-be creditors to review what other lenders have experienced with you as their client.

Banks still depend on their own ability to encourage from you the remaining details, as they can't review a complete picture solely from the credit bureau report. They need to get behind the information on the bureau report, while discovering the reasons behind the numbers that are only available through you, and what you say about them.

In a sales environment within a bank, it is also likely that they would not perform any extra diligence to search the title on your property to support your comments that you own it free-and-clear. They would simply make a note in your credit application that it was an earlier inheritance gift from your baby-boomer parents (or whatever your reason) and it is likely to not receive further attention so long as you don't attempt to pledge it as collateral.

Credit bureaus are evolving

Records from a variety of businesses and their information are gathered by credit bureaus. Financial institutions, retailers, and other credit issuers pay fees to belong to a credit bureau. They supply information about their customers as well as consult records of the bureau when considering their own applications for credit.

Credit bureaus (which are governed by provincial legislation) do not make the decision about whether a consumer receives credit. That's up to the lender. Credit bureaus only provide a historic picture, organizing all the reported repayment history available on an individual that has been collected over the years. Information can remain up to 20 years depending on what kind of information it is.

Their systems have evolved to include unbiased predictive scores to project a client's future credit risk, or potential fraud. These predictions are driven by the information their file contains on you. It also considers the number of times your file has been requested by creditors, how often your address has changed, your employment history, and any formal credit collection, judgment, or bankruptcy issues. They do not collect or exchange information regarding criminal records or charges.

As credit bureau systems and filters continue to evolve, lending institutions depend on them more and more when making decisions in their own lending processes.

 It doesn't matter what province you live in, or move to. There is only one file with each credit bureau agency that contains your information. Any address changes would be noted on the report.

Credit bureau agencies provide information to qualifying companies after being paid their fee. In some provinces, territories (and states) auto insurance companies now request a copy of your credit bureau report to determine if they should raise your premiums or not each year, or even keep you as an insured driver. By doing this they are making the assumption that if you poorly manage your credit rating, something extremely valuable to the health of your financial future, then perhaps you are an irresponsible driver and are at greater risk of having or causing an accident. If the information was incorrect on your credit report or out of date, your auto insurance rates could increase because of it. You must remain very alert that this type of financial profiling is not detrimental to you.

How to get a copy of your file

 Unless you request (pull) your own credit file report and verify each trade line, how can you be sure your credit history is accurate?

To obtain a copy of your credit file place a call to the primary bureaus or visit their web page for further information on your file. In some provinces, your credit file information can be given out over the phone or received by mail. The local bureau's telephone number is usually listed in the white pages of the telephone book.

You'll need proper identification and may be required to make your request in writing to assure your file is kept confidential. In most cases a copy of your credit report is available free of charge. If you're not comfortable under-standing how to read the information it contains, call to arrange an appointment to review your credit file with a representative of that bureau. It is important to review and proof the information it contains regularly. This helps prevent people with similar spellings to your name having their credit information mixed in with yours.

Personally, I would stay away from companies who advertise on the Internet a service, which monitors your credit rating for you. These services charge a fee for them to access and monitor your credit report for changes. If a change occurs you are notified by email. You're also able to monitor your report personally for changes any time you want during the period of time you have paid for through their web page. I prefer to call the bureaus myself, and monitor from the source. This way, I'm not completing personal information on a web page of a service provider I know nothing about, and would be difficult to prove it is legitimate. (Please review Chapter 19—Privacy And Security Of Your Personal Information, and Chapter 7—Identity Theft.)

 Inaccurate information collected from creditors will not be corrected on your file until you initiate the investigation.

How to correct an error

If there's a mistake in your file, challenge it. Most errors can be corrected by providing receipts to prove that you've made a payment, or by getting the bureau to check with the creditor. Simply fill out a form requesting the appropriate item be removed from your file making mention to any proof you have attached (send copies, not originals) to assist their confirmation of the error. Ask the credit bureau reporting the error what their processes is for dealing with it. You'll find they are more than willing to assist your understanding of their escalation process for correcting errors in your file.

Mistakes in credit files are often the result of information about someone else with a similar name to yours being placed in the wrong file, and of delays or poor information sent by a creditor to the bureau. Having said all that, creditors are also able to have judgments passed against you, (they sue you in small claims court and get a judgement) which could remain for up to 20 years on your personal credit file.

Though credit bureaus will gladly correct mistakes, they may also refuse to change your file if the creditor disagrees with the change you want. If this is the case for you, then an opportunity to file a statement of your version of the situation will be taken and placed in your file. The statement may explain that you failed to pay your bills because you were sick or unemployed, or that you were withholding payment to a supplier in dispute over the quality of an item or service. If your poor credit record is well deserved, then your options are more limited. Information is generally kept in your file for six years —

seven for a bankruptcy. Bank and other lender electronic application process scoring models *do not* take these situations into consideration. It is very likely that if your situation is similar to the one explained above your application will score poorly without further proof and discussion in person with a lender.

However, arrangements you have made with creditors to repay your debts can be reflected in your file. A person could request a creditor place a letter of reference in their credit file stating they're now paying bills on time. Do the research yourself. Obtain the necessary letters from creditors regarding errors and keep an up-to-date file of your own to back up your story.

CHAPTER 8

Do You Have
A Bad Credit History?

There is no quick fix for a bad credit history if it is accurate and well deserved. Only consistent, positive behaviour over time can re-establish your credit rating. If a lender is reviewing a poor credit history they try to establish how long ago it happened, what the reasons were behind the problem, and whether repayment history has stabilized since then. You may be asked to provide evidence the issues have been resolved, or the errors corrected.

Divorce is a common reason for the credit of some people to become destroyed. Some banks understand this to be beyond normal conditions, and see past it. How recent the derogatory information is can still hold you back from getting what you want. If your divorce happened two years ago, but since then you have paid all your loans and credit cards on time, you are well on your way to establishing a very positive credit profile.

I believe it's unlikely that a so-called credit-repair firm could do anything more to improve your credit file. Be wary of any individual or firm that promises it will fix a bad file if you pay them a fee. It would be too good to be true if they promised the miracle needed to clean up your record and turn you into an A-1 customer. A credit clinic cannot assist a consumer to have accurate and true information removed from a credit file. It is there and will remain so for a very good reason.

Carol-Lynn Lepard of Ontario's Consumer Ministry stated, "The Ministry has received complaints that credit-repair agencies collected money from customers but failed to perform a service." Lepard advises anyone with credit problems or concerns to consider seeking help from a local credit counselling service. In some provinces and territories, a branch of the provincial government offers this service.

A list of not-for-profit Credit Counselling Agencies is shown below for your convenience, which also can be found in your local telephone book listings:

Not-for-profit credit counselling agencies

Credit Counselling Society of British Columbia:
                          1-888-527-8999

Debtors Assistance Branch Ministry of Attorney General:
        (Only in BC): 1-800-663-7867
        Victoria: 250-387-1747
        Burnaby: 604-660-3550
        Kamloops: 250-828-4511

Credit Counselling Society of Alberta:
                          1-888-294-0076
        Calgary: 403-265-2201
        Edmonton: 403-423-5265

Department of Justice, Provincial Mediation Board
    Regina: 306-787-5387
    Saskatoon: 306-933-6520

Community Financial Counselling Services (Manitoba):
                     204-989-1900

Ontario Association of Credit Counselling Services:
                     1-888-746-3328

Personal Credit Counselling Services (NFL &
Labrador):   709-753-5812

Department of Community Affairs (PEI):
                     902-368-4580

Port Cities Debt Counselling Society (NS):
                     902-453-6510

Access Nova Scotia Department of Consumer Services:
                     1-800-670-4357

Credit Counselling Services of Atlantic Canada, Inc.
    (NB):   1-800-539-2227

Consumer Affairs Branch, Department of Justice:
    (NB):   506-453-2659

Family Services of Fredericton Inc.:
                     506-458-8211

Contact Consumer Services for a referral (Yukon):
                     867-667-5111

Consumer Services (NWT):
                     867-873-7125

CHAPTER 9

You Must Maintain
A Solid Credit Rating

These four tips will help you maintain a strong credit rating:

✔ **Know your financial worth**. It's impossible to plan and stay on a budget if you don't know how much money you have to work with. Know the source of all income, and have a tax planning strategy in place.

✔ **Get a tight grip of your expenses**. Analyse your spending habits, and keep track of where your money goes. No more impulse shopping! Include savings and / or RRSPs as an expense within your budget to help you save for retirement.

✔ **Pay off high interest debt first**. Think about consolidating high interest loans into one low interest loan or personal line of credit. Both usually carry lower interest rates, and you'll have one monthly payment to worry about. Try calling your lowest interest credit card company to transfer the balances on all your other credit cards to them to reduce interest costs. Sometimes card companies will offer lower interest rates on the portion you transfer in to them to compete for this business.

✔ **Don't keep your credit cards at their limits**. While it may be tempting to pay only the minimum each month, try paying off the balance to avoid interest charges. Keep a separate monthly list of who you pay interest to and how much, and see how quickly your concern grows to pay it off!

How your credit file is rated

Here are ratings typically found in a credit file. The credit grantor (bank, department store, oil company) issues the rating, not the credit bureau.

R0	Too new to rate; approved but not used
R1	Pays within 30 days of billing; or pays as agreed.
R2	Pays in more than 30 days but not more than 60; or is one payment past due.
R3	Pays in more than 60 days but not more than 90; or two payments past due.
R4	Pays in more than 90 days but not more than 120, or is three payments past due.
R5	Account is at least 120 days overdue but is not yet rated an R9.

R6	(This rating has not been assigned)
R7	Making regular payments under a consolidation order or similar arrangement.
R8	Repossession.
R9	Bad debt account placed for collection.

National Credit Bureaus contact numbers:

EQUIFAX 1-800-465-7166 (www.equifax.ca)
TRANSUNION 1-800-663-9980 (www.tuc.ca)

There is more information on your credit report than repayment history: collection items you've paid or neglected; every time you change your address; when your credit report is accessed that company's name is always logged. The more companies that access your credit report in the same period of time actually hurts your chances of getting approved. Don't become known as a credit seeker. As you shop at each bank for the best loan rates, each pull and review their copy of your credit report. They also know all the banks you've applied to, and are not able to determine if you're shopping for rates, or desperately need money and are applying everywhere. This is known as "shot gunning" for a loan and is not a good practice.

As your credit bureau report builds and updates with new information, a special model takes all the available data when requested and creates a score. Every time you move, apply for credit, miss payments, etc., your score may be affected. The poorer the score, the more risk is seen by financial institutions when lending to you so the more you shop for credit, the less chance of getting approved. Some lenders electronic application processes have built in filters that reference the bureaus' score for you in their application process, thus directly influencing the success of your application, though the score is not the sole factor influencing the success of your application.

A creditor reviewing your credit report, after seeing a few credit inquiries listed around the same time, may wonder why you were never approved. Perhaps this lender wonders were they missing something that the others didn't. As well, there is the risk that a few loans could be granted all at the same time in isolation from each other. That is to say that the other creditors were unaware of the other applications status (approved / declined) and you could very well be leveraged beyond your limits if all those loans were approved. Some people do this, and not only hurt themselves as they can't repay their commitments, but their credit score and file will now be compromised due to their own poor judgement as a borrower the next time they need financing.

As discussed before, a credit card provider that regularly increases your limits ties up your borrowing power. Sometimes on your credit report the card limit is not reported, only your highest balance. This means that if you have a card approved maximum limit of $10,000 and have never put more than $4,000 on it, the trade line could actually be read as having a $4,000 credit card. If you only use $4,000 on your card, then reduce the limit to be the same and *formally* free up your borrowing power for future needs.

I have included for your convenience a copy of the training guide that a credit bureau, *TransUnion of Canada*,

Inc., provides to lenders that helps explain how to read their reports, understand formats and other information contained within each person's credit file. If you have further questions on how to interpret the information in your credit file with TransUnion, call them direct for further explanation or visit their web page (captioned above). Also, it would be prudent to review the information Equifax has collected on you as well to ensure they are current. Banks use one, the other, and sometimes both bureaus report when trying to make a decision of lending to you.

TransUnion Training Guide

The author wishes to thank TransUnion of Canada Inc. for permitting the use of their bank-training manual in this publication, to assist you in the understanding of your credit report. They encourage your direct contact with them for further clarification, or to provide answers to your questions.

TransUnion.

Credit Report
Training Guide

May 2002

Trans Union of Canada, Inc.
Consumer Credit Report

Date 01 May 2002

❶	Surname	Given Name(s)	Soc. Ins. No.	Birth
Subject	Consumer	Robert/B	### ### ###	11Oct1958
Spouse	Consumer	Jane/B	### ### ###	22Jan1963
AKA	Consumer	Brian/Robert		

On File	Last Inq		Telephone	Prev Phone
20Jul1994	01May2002		4165551212	9055551212

RESIDENCE(S)

Street	City	Prov	Postal	Since	Cnfrm
123 Main Street, Apt. 101	Anytown	ON	M1M 1M1	01Dec1994	01Nov1999
456 Back Street	Newtown	ON	L1L 1L1	01Jul1990	01April1994

EMPLOYMENT(S)

Employer's Name & Address		Occupation	Since	Cnfrm
National Steel Car Oakville ON		Welder	01Nov1990	01Aug1998
Spouse's Employer				
Henry's Hot Dogs/111 Nathan St, Toronto		Cashier	01Dec1992	01Jul1993

❷ **FILE SUMMARY**

Legals=1-Jan1999	Bkrp=1-Dec1997	Coll=2-Mar2001	Inqs=2-May2002	6Mnth=1	CollInq=0
High=$9500	Baln=$3310	PDue=$0	Paym=$310	Acct=3	Neg=2	Paid=1
Trade=Jul1994/May1998	Balances	Inst=$2352	Rev=$958	Open=$0	Mort=$0	#Reg=1

❸ **MESSAGES**

| **Trans Alert** | INPUT DOB DOES NOT MATCH FILE DOB |
| **Hawk Alert** | INPUT SUBJECT SIN IS INVALID |

❹ **BUREAU RISK SCORE**

Empirica: 618 **ALERT**

Factors 38 Serious delinquency AND derogatory public record or collection filed
15 Lack of recent bankcard account information
18 Frequent delinquency
12 Length of time revolving/open accounts have been established

Horizon 651 **ALERT**

Factors 38 Serious delinquency, and public record or collection filed
20 Length of time since derogatory public record or collection filed
16 lack of recent revolving account information
18 Number of accounts with delinquency

TransRisk (optional)
RPM (optional)

❺ **TRADE**

Rept	Open	Last	H. Credit	Balance	PastDue	Terms	Payment Pattern 30/60/90/#M	MOP
DC	DEPARTMENT STORE						99999999954321111111111111	
Sep1998	Apr1995	Sep1998	1000	958	0	0/M	1 1 11 44	R9
	INCL IN BANKRUPTCY							
OC	OIL COMPANY						99999543211111111111111	
Jul1999	Jul1994	Jul1999	1000	0	0	0/M	1 1 7 60	O9
	THIRD PARTY COLLECTIONS							
BB	CANADIAN BANK, 5195551212						11111111111111XXXXX111111	
May2002	May1998	May2002	7500	2352	0	310/M	0 0 0 48	I1
		JOINT						
BB		May2002	175000	135000	0	870M	11111211XXXXXXXXXXXXXXXX	
May2002		JOINT						M1

❻ **REGISTERED ITEMS**

Reptd	Open	Matur	Amount	Balance	Pastdue	Terms	Security
ZZ	A NATIONAL BANK, 130 Dundas Street E. Mississauga, ON						A E
Jan1998	Jan1998	Dec2001					

❼ **BANKRUPTCY**

Rvsd	Reptd	Trustee	Assets	Liab
Nov1998	Dec1997	BURT HOWE	500	75520
		HOWE & ASSOCIATES	DISCHARGED Sept1998	
		12 MAIN ST., HAMILTON	JOINT	
		Court 12345		

❽ **LEGAL ITEMS**

Rvsd	Reptd	Plaintiff's Name	Amount	Balance
Sep1999	Jan1999	AB	1500	0
		HAMILTON	PAID Jul1999	
		JUDG 321321		

❾ **COLLECTIONS**

Rvsd	Reptd	Agency/Creditor's Name	Amount	Balance
Sept1999	July1999	GAS COMPANY	577	0
			PAID Sept1999	
Sept2001	Mar2001	CABLE COMPANY	404	404
			STILL OWING Sept2001	

❿ **INQUIRIES**

Date	Credit Grantor	
01May2002	BB Bank	4035551212
25 Nov1999	DC Department Store	6045551212

⓫ **REMARKS**

Date	CONFIRMED VICTIM STATEMENT
30Dec1997	#HK# Confirmed fraud victim; before extending credit verify all applicant information. Contact me for verification at home: (XXX)XXX-XXXX or work: (XXX)XXX-XXXX. Dated XX/XXXX

This completes the file for ROBERT CONSUMER.

TransUnion Training Guide page 2

CREDIT REPORT FIELDS

1 FILE AND DEMOGRAPHIC INFORMATION
- Date the credit report was issued
- Consumer's and spouse's name, plus any known aliases
- Social Insurance Number for consumer and spouse
- Date of birth, telephone number, current and previous employment
- Date the file was created
- Last date of inquiry on file
- Current address and date reported
- All previous addresses on our file

2 FILE SUMMARY

Provides a snapshot of all activity on the consumer's credit report

From left to right in the first row
- Total number of legal items; with date of most current
- Total number of bankruptcies; with date of most current
- Total number of collections; with date of most current
- Total number of inquiries; with date of most current
- Number of inquiries in last six months
- Number of inquiries that are collection inquiries; in the last 24 months

From left to right in the second row
- Total high credit to the consumer
- Running balance on the available credit
- Total past due
- Total payments
- Number of accounts
- Number of accounts that have negative rating (MOP of 3,4,5,7,8,9)
- Number of accounts paid

From left to right in the third row
- Date of oldest account opened and date of most current account opened
- Breakdown of total running balances – Installment, Revolving, Open, Mortgage
- Total number of Registered Items

3 SPECIAL MESSAGES

Highlights specific credit file conditions that may include:
- A TransAlert® message: appears if current input address does not match any addresses on returned file, if input Social Insurance Number does not match the file Social Insurance Number; if there are four or more inquiries within the last 60 days, or if the input surname does not match returned file.
- A HAWK® message (optional): The information in the inquiry is compared against information of known and potential frauds. If a match occurs against the input address, phone number or SIN, a warning message is generated prompting further investigation.

4 BUREAU RISK SCORE

EMPIRICA® (optional) displays unbiased predictive score to project a consumer's future credit risk. It is displayed numerically with four explanation factors. These factors are displayed in order based on their relative impact on the final score. An *Alert* message occurs when a credit file contains MOP 7 or greater, a negative public record, a collection, or previous bankruptcy.

HORIZON® (optional) The HORIZON® is a bankruptcy loss ratio model.

RAVEN® (optional) The RAVEN® model rank orders applications by their likelihood of being fraudulent.

TransRisk (optional) TransRisk is a general risk score designed for account management uses.

RPM (optional) RPM is a revenue projection model.

5 TRADES

Provides an ongoing historical and current record of the consumer's buying and payment activities. Trade information includes the following
- Industry Code
- Name and telephone number of credit grantor
- Date the credit information was reported to TransUnion
- Date the account was opened
- Date of last activity on the account
- The high credit or credit limit on the account
- Balance owing as of date reported
- Amount past due as of date reported
- Terms of payment showing the dollar amount owing and payment frequency
  Frequency codes are:

E – Bi Monthly	M – Monthly
D – Daily	S – Semi Annually
Q – Quarterly	Y – Annually
W – Weekly	B – Bi Weekly

- Payment pattern gives a detailed history of payment ratings for a maximum of 24 months. It reads from left to right with the most current verified entry on the left on the first line. The line below gives a summary of the historical status of the ratings for the total number of months the credit grantor has been reviewing the account. There are buckets for 30, 60 and 90 days. "X" = months with no rating reported. Ratings of "2" are added to the 30-day bucket, ratings of "3" are in the 60-day bucket and all other ratings (4,5,7,8,9) are counted in the 90-day bucket. #M is the total of months reviewed.
- Type of account (R,I,O,M) and Manner Of Payment at which the account is currently reported. (See breakdown of MOP codes for more details.)

R – Revolving	I – Installment
O – Open	M – Mortgage

- A narrative is used if the account is in some type of dispute or requires an explanation of the credit condition of the account.
- For mortgage information, the name and telephone number of the credit grantor are not displayed. The open date is not displayed.

6 REGISTERED ITEMS

This item is NOT RATED gives full detail of registration including security
A – Consumer Goods B – Inventory C – Equipment
D – Assignment of book debts E – Other securities

7 BANKRUPTCY AND/OR PROPOSAL

Will be maintained on consumer's file in compliance with provincial regulations. Includes: date reported, name and address of trustees, assets, liabilities, date revised and discharges with date.

8 LEGAL ITEMS

Will be maintained on consumer's file in compliance with provincial regulations. Includes: date reported, plaintiff's name, court, amount, balance, comments and revised date.

9 COLLECTION INFORMATION

Will be maintained on consumer's file in compliance with provincial regulations. Includes agency name and creditor's names (if provided), amount, balance and comments, plus date reported and/or revised date.

10 INQUIRIES

Displays the users who have viewed the consumer's credit file. Includes the date of the inquiry, the industry code of the inquirer, their name and telephone number.

11 REMARKS

Consumer statement allows for comments from the consumer regarding information on their file.

CREDIT REPORT CODES

INDUSTRY CODE CLASSIFICATION

CODE	KIND OF BUSINESS
A	Automotive
B	Banks & Trust Companies
C	Clothing
D	Department/Retail
F	Finance, Personal
G	Grocery
H	Home Furnishings
I	Insurance
J	Jewelry
K	Contractors
L	Lumber, Building Material, Hardware
M	Medical & Related Health
N	Credit Card & Travel/Entertainment
O	Oil Companies
P	Personal Service Other than Medical
Q	Finance Companies Other than Personal Finance
R	Real Estate & Public Accommodations
S	Sporting Goods
T	Farm & Garden Suppliers
U	Utilities & Fuel
V	Government
W	Wholesale
X	Advertising
Y	Collection Services
Z	Miscellaneous

TYPES OF ACCOUNTS

Open Account
(payment required in full) . . . . O
Revolving or Option (30 days) . . . . R
Installment
(fixed number of payments) I
Mortgage . . . . M

USUAL MANNER OF PAYMENT

	Type of Account		
	O	R	I
Too new to rate; approved, but not used	0	0	0
Pays (or paid) within 30 days of billing; pays account as agreed	1	1	1
Pays (or paid) in more than 30 days, but not more than one payment past due	2	2	2
Pays (or paid) in more than 60 days but not more than 90 days, or two payments past due	3	3	3
Pays (or paid) in more than 90 days, but not more than 120 days, or three or more payments past due	4	4	4
Account is at least 120 days overdue but is not yet rated a "9"	5	5	5
Making regular payments under a consolidation order or similar arrangement	7	7	7
Repossession	8	8	8
Bad debt, placed for collection; skip	9	9	9

Trans**Union**.

325 Milner Avenue, Suite 1501
Toronto, Ontario M1B 5N1
Tel: 416 609-2070
Customer Service: 1 800 565-2280
Fax: 1 905 527-8020
www.tuc.ca

A member of The Marmon Group of companies

10k
SM001E 05/02

For the name and address of your nearest TransUnion representative, see below or call 416 609-2070. Your local TransUnion bureau is:

TransUnion Training Guide page 4

Don't Borrow Money Until You Read This Book! 63

CHAPTER 10

Your Income and How You Should Report It

People who aren't self-employed receive at the end of the year an income receipt (T4) slip from their employer(s). They complete their T1General Personal Tax Return then submit it to Canada Customs and Revenue Agency. They either pay additional tax or enjoy a moderate refund. It is through this income reporting that lenders verify the amount of income you receive throughout the year as being true. The theory being that when the government has accepted what you've reported, it must be true or you would be audited.

Understanding that financial institutions place such a high value on your tax return means you should take time to understand the tax system as best you can. Purchase a book or speak with a tax consultant to review your options. Learn to maximize every benefit available in the annual tax process you qualify for. Find a balance in the amount of income you report each year and your related expenses / allowable deductions. Taxes continue to be our biggest single-most expense, often outdoing our mortgage, and it's worth the time to properly understand where all our hard-earned money is going.

You may have heard people operate a small business

for tax reasons, but what does that really mean? The answer can be as complicated as you like, but in an effort to keep things simple, I'll try to outline the general concept here of a sole ownership. Owning a business costs you money to operate. You need to purchase supplies, pay utilities for the space you occupy, even if it's only a room in your home, additional labour expenses as well as vehicle costs. If you own a small business you're also generating an income (CCRA states they assume, as you do / should, are operating the business to make a profit). It is conceivable you're likely to lose money from time to time depending on the market conditions and the effort you put into your business. Some sole proprietors show losses related to one-time expense items (a large purchase or repair) that is not expected to be repeated again.

If your income from business is a negative amount after these deductions you'll find that you're able to reduce the amount of tax you pay from your regular salaried employment. (See a tax planner, chartered accountant or bookkeeper for more in-depth overview than presented here if you are not familiar with this concept).

The trick is to have expenses that lenders are willing to add back into your income. As reviewed earlier, these include depreciation/amortization, capital cost allowance, interest and one-time expenses (most of which don't actually use up cash). If done correctly, the value of these items can be added back to your available income to service debt.

Banks consider debt to be repaid only through cash availability. The more available, the more debt can be serviced. The stronger your borrowing power, the more preferred a client you become.

A common error usually seen with sole proprietors is they don't properly research what expense items a bank will add back to their income. In doing so, they fail to weigh expenses against reserving some income to service debt. When it comes time to apply for credit they discover they have merely expensed items for tax purposes and are unable to include these items back to service debt as first thought. Though they have reduced the amount of tax they are required to pay to CCRA, they have not reserved enough income to service debt, which negatively impacts their TDS and GDS ratios. They have in effect, reduced their borrowing power relative to reducing their income for tax purposes.

People interpret tax rules differently. Bending the rules to interpretation is very different from breaking them, and not all rules can be bent to serve your purpose. At the end of the day, if you're unable to convince CCRA to your perception of their rule in an audit situation, you will be required to pay the tax owed to them along with any interest penalties. After CCRA's decision demanding you to repay tax, the amount could appear on your credit bureau report as a collection item. CCRA could also garnishee your salary until they receive all that is due to them.

Having said that, tax department employees are very willing, in most circumstances, to negotiate scheduled repayment terms with you as long as you meet the commitments you make with them. If you find yourself in a poor situation such as this, be upfront and forth-coming with CCRA staff and they will be more willing to work with you. Ignorance is no excuse with CCRA. It is wiser to seek professional tax advice in the beginning than to have to repay the government back taxes with interest penalties and possibly receive a bad mark on your credit report.

Most people, when asked, will say their biggest expense in their lives is their mortgage. That's not entirely true, and the government is happy that most of us have this perception. Our biggest expense is actually the amount of tax we pay. We're taxed when we earn money working hard to build the economy and we're taxed when we spend it trying hard to support our economy through shopping. Understanding this may encourage you to think about the amount of tax you pay, and how to reduce it.

 Remain focused on strengthening your borrowing power while tax planning. Use expense items banks will add back to your total income.

Another reason financial institutions rely heavily on your tax return to prove income is the notice of assessment created by the federal government and sent to you also shows when you owe back taxes. If they are owed from prior years, pay them before going for a loan or mortgage and be ready to prove you have done it. Banks rarely lend to those in a tax arrears position. If you can't pay the government, it's likely that you can't pay a bank loan either; not to mention the federal government has access to your personal assets before all others. They get paid first, before banks, before anybody.

It may be prudent in your situation to request your employer to deduct more tax from each pay cheque for submission to CCRA. This can be done through your Human Resource office, and has benefits.

You're in control of the amount of tax being paid on your income throughout the year, verses waiting to year end to determine if you owe additional taxes or not, which may place you further in debt.

You're using the government as a way to force yourself to save, predicting you will have contributed too much tax and will receive a refund at the end of the year. Though this does not accumulate interest, it does force you to save. Be sure to put the refund in an RRSP, or pay off a loan to receive the full benefit. Don't fritter the refund away as it can provide you with a debt-free future when you handle your affairs properly

Commissioned sales people

When you are a commissioned sales person, your income will be reviewed more intensely by the lenders. You will be required to show at least three years of income verification (tax returns with their notice of assessments). Your yearly commission income will be considered by using an overall average of those three consecutive years. If you had a big income year and want to buy a new car, remember the commissions of the two previous years will be added to the one great year you just had, and it is the average of these three years that will be used to calculate the cash you have available to service the new loan you're applying.

Cash is the only thing that services debt payments. Not a co-signer, or a strong guarantee from someone you know. It's so important to understand the way to properly present how much cash you have each month, and the type of debt you service each month.

$ $ $

Financial institutions don't care that you may be a great person, and just need a break. Their job is to focus on minimizing the risk of you not being able to repay your loan, on time.

CHAPTER 11

Live Within Your Means

If you don't have it, don't spend it. If you're going to charge something to your credit card and not pay within 30 days, it's better not to have the item in the first place. Why borrow and pay interest on an item at 20 – 30% per year when you can do without?

Pay heed to this general warning!

If you project a lifestyle you can't afford so others will see only the successful side of you, you're going to be much more embarrassed when you think through how having a bankruptcy makes you look when you're in over your head. The golden rule to live by is to live within your means and not fond hope. Are you buying merely to acquire or is it needed!

Review TDS (total debt service) and GDS (gross debt service) definitions, as these are the very ratios financial institutions seek when they analyse how much debt you're able to afford. When you understand these two basic ratios then position your lifestyle to reflect them. Give banks a reason to want to lend to you. Decide for yourself whether you want the lending service they are trying to sell you. You are the consumer after all and have a choice to acquire not only the type of lending, but also from whom you buy it. With a strong GDS, TDS and credit rating, lenders will line up for your business. What does this mean to you? Well, you're now in a position of authority, and have more leverage while negotiating terms and interest rates as you're viewed to be a preferred client.

Who's a preferred client? Someone with a strong credit bureau report, money in their savings account, control of their expenses (stable GDS and TDS), steady employment and doing business with them in some way (chequing account, credit card, RRSP etc.) that they have confidence with them as their client.

 Don't let this apply to you. "Let us all be happy and live within our means, even if it means we have to borrow the money to do it with."

– Natural History.

Banks will buy business from preferred clients through negotiating better and lower terms, lower interest rates, and security. Commonly these are referred to as *safe* loans, and banks charge less interest as the risk of not being repaid is marginal, or safe.

Are you positioning your financial affairs to be a preferred client? Why not start today!

Review the four tips in the section of Chapter 9 to help you maintain a strong credit rating so that you live within your means. It's a lot less stressful. Who doesn't want a happier life?

Complete your personal Income and Expense sheet

Special types of income, and their leverage power

People with unique income streams often wonder how much a financial institution will value it when considering repayment of a loan or mortgage. Below I give general indications of their leverage power, though each bank will review your unique source of income differently depending on your need. You should call ahead and inquire directly with your bank to understand how they will view your circumstances.

Foreign employees working in Canada …
   a) It may depend on what type of financing you're looking for that will dictate your qualifications and income leverage strength. It would be best to apply for any kind of financing within your first twelve months of relocating or immigrating to Canada.
   b) Let the lender know if your company also provides a housing subsidy in addition to your regular wage or salary.
   c) There may be a minimum salary range they are looking for to qualify your application, but I would anticipate once it has been established that they are comfortable with you, your employer and salary range, that they would consider 100% of it in normal circumstances.
   d) If you are paid in US funds, a conversion rate of about 40% will be used.

Child support and alimony income ...

a) You may be required to prove you have received these payments for more than a year, and provide a copy of your T1-General tax return detailing amounts.

b) A copy of your separation agreement or divorce may also be requested to understand how long payments are to continue, and their amounts or special conditions.

c) In most cases 100% of the amount should be considered. A smaller percentage may be considered if it is your only source of income.

Foster care income ...

a) This form of income will be averaged over last three years (similar to commissioned employees) and the lower of the average or the last year's total income amount from this source will be used.

b) Your experience will be reviewed, and minimum tenure may be expected of two years before accepting this form of income stream in any debt-servicing calculation.

c) A letter from your agency confirming you're an approved foster caregiver, being verified as currently approved to act in this capacity, may also be requested.

d) If your foster care income represents more than 50% of your total income, there may be ceilings on how much money you're able to borrow when applying for a mortgage, or restrictions in having a mortgage insured.

e) There may also be a requirement confirming the maximum number of children in your care does not exceed the legal limit.

Self-employment, over-time, commission, and seasonal income …

a) An average is calculated using the last three years confirmed income amounts.
b) 100% of the average or recent year (whichever is lower) is eligible to service debt.
c) Evidence will be required to establish a three-year trend.
d) If you have seasonal income, they may want to confirm less than 30% of it comes from unemployment insurance benefits.

Part-time income …

a) 100% may be used in most cases, though sometimes provided it does not represent more than 25% of your total income.
b) A minimum of two-years stability may need to be demonstrated through T4 slips and your notice of assessment in order for it to be considered.

Maternity leave income …

a) 100% of the estimated return-to-work income should be considered.
b) A letter from your employer detailing your return date, expected salary and position will be required.

c) If a letter cannot be obtained, a lower percentage will be used, or this income may be discounted entirely as it cannot be confirmed.

Rental income ...

a) Though this form of income will be considered to service debt, the expenses and upkeep on your income property will also use up this income stream's leveraging power. Taxes, utilities, repairs and maintenance are expenses that these incomes will likely service.

b) A 5% vacancy rate may also be considered as an expense you will need to cover. This percentage assumes that 5% of your rental income will be used to cover expenses when the property is not rented out, or earning income.

Pension and disability income ...

a) Please review Chapter 11, fixed-income borrowers.

 Spouses share some assets, liabilities, income sources and expense items. Try completing a summary for each individual, then consolidate all information into a final grand summary to avoid counting things twice.

Calculating your total gross annual income

Primary Employment Income, Annual Salary, or Wages	$_____
Secondary Employment Income, Annual Salary, or Wages	$_____
Commissions	$_____
Overtime	$_____
Bonuses	$_____
RRIF (Registered Retirement Income Fund)	$_____
Dividend or Interest Income – (non registered)	$_____
Rental Income	$_____
Alimony, Child Support or Maintenance Payments Received	$_____
Other Income	$_____
Other Income	$_____
Total Gross Annual Income	$_____

 Also complete this table using your NET income from all sources. Doing this creates a budget using actual cash you have available each year, then break down this budget monthly to help stay on track day-to-day.

Calculating your total annual expenses

*(see following page re explanation for * and **)*

Tithing $ _____ *

Mortgage Payments $ _____

Rental Payments $ _____

Real Estate Taxes (current portion) $ _____

Real Estate Taxes (past due portion) $ _____ **

Annual Natural Gas, Oil,
   or Propane Costs $ _____
Annual Electrical Costs $ _____

Annual Communication Costs
   (phone, cable, satellite, internet, etc.) $ _____ *

Groceries (consider your weekly
   average cost, and multiply by 52 weeks) $ _____ *

Personal Taxes due (or past due) $ _____ **

Alimony, Child Support,
   or Maintenance payments $ _____

Insurance Premiums
   (car, home, contents, etc.) $ _____ *

Insurance Premiums (life) $ _____ *

Consumer Loan #1
   (total annual payments) $ _____

Consumer Loan #2
   (total annual payments) $ _____

Vehicle Loan / Lease #1
   (total annual payments) $ _____

Vehicle Loan / Lease #2
   (total annual payments) $ _____

Vehicle (consider year of vehicle in your
   estimate for repairs and maintenance) $ _____ *

Vehicle Fuel and Oil Costs $ _____ *

Recreational Vehicle Loan Payment $ _____

Credit Cards (portion you plan to
   reduce on carry-forward balances) $ _____ *,**

Lines Of Credit (portion you plan to
   reduce on carry-forward balances) $ _____ *,**

RRSP Contributions (personal)	$ _____	*
RRSP Contributions (spousal)	$ _____	*
Savings contribution for first child's education / wedding	$ _____	*
Savings contribution for second child's education / wedding	$ _____	*
Health Expenses (prescriptions, dental, medical, counselling, massage, etc.)	$ _____	*
Children Activities (clubs, memberships, special activities, etc.)	$ _____	*
Entertainment (movies, seasonal passes, vacation, etc)	$ _____	*
Other	$ _____	
Other	$ _____	
Total Annual Expenses	$ _____	

 Complete this table using monthly totals too. This helps create your budget when coupled with your NET total monthly income statement. At the end of the day, if you spend only what you have, you're well on your way to being responsible with your cash flow, and maintaining a strong credit file! (Make necessary changes if you find you don't have enough NET cash to service your monthly expenses.)

*   These are items financial institutions usually won't enquire about when considering your debt servicing for a new loan, but you should be aware how they affect your overall financial picture. Some of these items can encourage a financial institution to compete for your business, like RRSPs. Ask them what products they have to compete with the one you have as part of your loan application process / client interview. Entice them that there is potentially more business from you!

**   These are items that have tangible interest costs attached to them which are difficult to capture, though keep in mind you must pay this fluctuating interest cost throughout the year depending on the balance outstanding at time interest is calculated. It would be prudent to not carry a balance on your credit cards and lines of credit, and to keep your taxes current and avoid this expense altogether.

Fixed income borrowers

For fixed income and/or disability income a few points are worth remembering. Though it may be difficult to budget monthly to live properly let alone service a new loan, banks accept this income as being as secure as steady employment, depending on your circumstances. If you can service the loan and remain within their lending ratios (GDS and TDS) you're very likely to receive that loan. Commonly people on fixed incomes assume they automatically don't qualify. That is a myth. Think of it this way; If you have the cash flow available to service the debt, and it's a proven source of income why wouldn't someone want to take a risk and lend to you? Perhaps they wouldn't if your credit rating is poor. Perhaps your fixed income may expire or is conditional on some other commitments? When in doubt, arrange an appointment with your branch to ask the loans officer, "What would it take for me to secure a new loan through your bank?" They'll tell you exactly where you stand.

 Gross income can be considered when it is not taxed at the source. Income may be calculated on a gross-up base (to return to the gross amount of income before taxes deducted), which means adding back the amount of tax (estimating 25%) already deducted, as CCRA will refund this amount when you do your annual income tax return. Example: ($500.00 a month x 1.25) x 12 months.

In cases of disability income you will be required to prove income is long-term and guaranteed for the duration of your life if applying for a mortgage.

 Don't forget to pull your own credit bureau report, and plan your budget as shown earlier, to know where you are financially, prior to making your appointment.

CHAPTER 12

Finding The Balance Between Your Liabilities And Assets

As most business owners understand, it is important to have a balance between the amount of money owed, to the value of the asset owned. For a business, this is the financial balance between assets, liabilities and equity. So for our personal lives, we must be aware of our financial balance, and that it not become an imbalance.

Your Personal Statement Of Affairs (PSOA) is your balance sheet. Savings are an asset (cash, RRSP, GIC, stock, etc.) as well as the portion of your home that has been repaid coupled with its market equity (the amount it is worth if it was sold today, not what you paid for it).

Other assets include art, jewellery and chattels (cars, boats, recreation vehicles, house trailers etc.). These asset classes don't carry as much weight toward your overall net worth as the first few. Don't fool yourself about your worth! Divide a piece of paper with two vertical lines. Head the left column "$ income at top value" as if you meant to sell the asset off, in the centre list the item. Call the right column, "lowest acceptable price," and then observe how quickly your material items add to your overall net worth.

Your debts or liabilities are: loans, mortgages, lines of credit, credit cards, and any lease or rental payments you're paying. Credit cards hold the potential to be maximized at any time, and as such just noting the balance is not enough. You need to identify the limits of each card.

In most cases you're able to match each debt you have with a corresponding asset (i.e., a car loan with a car). The balance slowly tips negative because of the more debt you have that can't be linked to a corresponding asset. This suggests that the cash you acquired through financing has been used as disposable income, or that you spent it on things you can't show as a resalable asset. That's not to say that if you have savings enough to offset the amount you owe in debt that you wouldn't be closer to a balance, even though you have borrowed cash to invest in your savings. It is certainly <u>not</u> a good idea if you're paying interest on a loan that's more than the amount of return you're getting in your savings vehicle (GICs, Canadian Savings Bonds, etc.).

Investing is an altogether different issue that needs to be reviewed with a licensed professional (investment advisor) if you're not confident that you can make educated decisions on your own. Poor investment advice can have significant negative impact on your credit rating if you "buy on margin," i.e., borrow only a percentage of the funds required for equity purchases and are unable to pay margin "calls" (the lender requesting immediate full repayment of the money on margin); or take out a loan to make an investment then find you're unable to repay the loan.

Your bank employs licensed staff willing to advise on various investment products and strategies. Nowadays they hold an arsenal of products to win over your business, and aren't commonly limited to their own brand name of products. If they sell only their products, switching banks is a good idea if you want to receive the investment advice your investment needs require. The benefit of going to your bank for financial advice is it's usually free. If your needs are more complex they may refer you to other types of specialists who may charge a fee but most needs can be met at a branch level without additional cost. Booking an appointment will help position you to be served by an experienced person verses walking in to meet with a person available who may not be the most experienced.

Aside from business lending, I recommend you review your own debt to equity and be comfortable about the direction in which you're moving. Does your debt tend to continually increase while your asset growth remains flat? This should be a red flag for you, as lenders certainly place value on determining their risk in lending to you through this ratio, and so should you in positioning your affairs. If the amount of debt you have exceeds your assets significantly, you will have difficulty adding more debt to a bad situation. You may also be in a position of having a low net worth, or even negative if this isn't managed well. With a negative net worth it is unlikely that a credit card application would be approved. A loan application may still be approved with a negative net worth if its purpose is to purchase an asset worth the same or more so you don't erode your net worth further.

What does all this mean to you? For starters make sure you want the debt in the first place, and it fills a purpose in your financial plan other than acquiring just for the sake of having it (or getting a free pen set to list how bad off you have become).

Complete your personal balance sheet

 If you lease your vehicle don't state the total resale value as an asset, rather only the portion (if any) you would receive if you returned the vehicle to the dealer. This could be a portion of your down payment.

Assets

Cash in all personal chequing and saving accounts	$_____
Saving for first child's education / wedding	$_____
Saving for second child's education / wedding	$_____
Additional Children savings	$_____
RRSP balance (personal only, spousal RRSP is registered as spouse's)	$_____
Marketable Securities (non-registered)	$_____
Life Insurance Policies (only cash surrender value)	$_____
Loan Receivables (money lent to other people owed back to you)	$_____
Mortgage Receivables (private mortgages	$_____
Real Estate / Principal Home (current market or appraised value)	$_____
Real Estate / Cottage (current market or appraised value)	$_____
Real Estate / Income Property (current market or appraised value)	$_____

Vehicle #1
    Make   Model   Year $ _____

Vehicle #2
    Make   Model   Year $ _____

Recreational Vehicle #1
    Make   Year $ _____

Recreational Vehicle #2
    Make   Year $ _____

Business Interests (any personal investment
    you have made to a business) $ _____

Other Assets $ _____

Other Assets $ _____

Other Assets $ ========

Total Assets $ _____

Liabilities

Consumer Loan #1 (balance owing) $ _____

Consumer Loan #2 (balance owing) $ _____

Vehicle Loan / Lease #1
    (balance owing / or payments left
    on lease term) $ _____

Vehicle Loan / Lease #2 (balance owing /
    or payments left on lease term) $ _____

Recreational Vehicle Loan
    (balance owing) $ _____

Real Estate / Principal Home
    (outstanding mortgage amount) $ _____

Real Estate / Cottage
    (outstanding mortgage amount) $ _____

Real Estate / Income Property
    (outstanding mortgage amount) $ _____

Credit Card #1
    Name of card (balance owing) $ _____

Credit Card #2 Name of card (balance owing)	$_____
Credit Card #3 Name of card (balance owing)	$_____
Credit Card #4 Name of card (balance owing)	$_____
Line Of Credit #1 (balance owing)	$_____
Line Of Credit #2 (balance owing)	$_____
Other Obligations	$_____
Other Obligations	$_____
Total Liabilities	$_____

Note: Though credit card and line of credit balances are current liabilities, financial institutions will want to know the authorized amount of each limit, as you do reserve the right to maximize them, creating more liability than your balances reflect today. Note your total authorized amount for these items in the margin for easy reference.

Calculating your total net worth

Calculating your net worth isn't as hard as it may appear. Simply carry the numbers over from your balance sheet totals into the small table below to see how much you're worth!

Total Assets		$_____
Total Liabilities	(minus)	($=========)
Total Net Worth		$_____

Calculating your tangible net worth

Calculating your tangible net worth paints a more realistic picture as it considers certain facts that are easily overlooked. Financial institutions will take your net worth value and drill it down until they understand your actual, or tangible, net worth.

For example: if you had to cash out your RRSP to access cash, withholding taxes would be deducted from the total. Your tangible RRSP value actually is lower than your invested amount, in relation to the withholding taxes you would be required to pay if you cashed out early. Financial institutions typically divide in half the value you indicate under RRSP on your balance sheet under assets to estimate their tangible value.

As you determine your tangible net worth, also consider if you had to sell your car or boat, how much cash could you realistically get? Financial institutions typically will deduct the full value of your cars and boats from your net worth statement. Not only do they not want to own these items if they were trying to get paid out and that's all you had to offer, but it's too costly to exercise security rights for a depreciated vehicle, organize a power of sale on the item, pay all the fees to do that, and keep what's left. It's more efficient to simply discount these items, along with house contents, tools, art, jewellery and other similar assets from your available net worth.

Private loans and mortgages you have with other individuals should also be deducted from your net worth as you continue to drill down to determine your tangible net worth. The perception that private loans are high risk dictates they should be discounted in part or in all from your total net worth. You may disagree, and that's okay, but a financial institution will discount these assets in value when determining your tangible net worth.

You may be surprised to discover the primary assets financial institutions value are limited to the equity in real property, investments, some of your RRSP's and cash. Having said that, some lenders may discount the cash amount you have indicated as an asset perceiving that it is the most liquid and could disappear the fastest in a desperate situation, and may discount your cottage value thinking it will be difficult to sell if you required cash quickly.

So, what is your tangible *net worth?*

Tangible net worth worksheet

Total Assets $_____

   Minus:

      50% of RRSP $_____

      Vehicle Values $_____

      Private Loans $_____

      Private Mortgages $_____

      House Contents $_____

      Jewelry / Art $_____

      Tools $_____

      Cash $_____

      Other Intangibles $_____

Total Intangibles $_____ — ($_____)

Total Liabilities   (minus) ($_____)

Total Tangible Net Worth $_____

When applying for a mortgage

When shopping for your mortgage, do *not* ask the lender to figure out the maximum mortgage you can afford, so you can buy the biggest house possible! There is a terrible risk facing you when you let your ego lead you into doing this. You may lose what is important to you, your wonderful, ideal family house, when you can't afford the upkeep of your lifestyle. You should know how much you could afford, don't ask someone else.

Consider this: Lenders have sales targets to meet and will likely use every bit of borrowing power you have to sell you a bigger mortgage, bringing them closer to their sales targets. Mortgage specialists and mortgage brokers are paid a commission on the amount of mortgages you are approved for, which means both lenders and brokers are focused on their own needs far more than yours, as they are motivated by different objectives than you. You're motivated to go to them to buy a house. They're motivated by salaries, awards and bonuses to sell as much debt as possible to qualified individuals.

 Never give away the financial cushion of having less debt to pay when bad times arrive. It could be all the difference it takes to keep your home!

You may qualify for that bigger mortgage. While the lender or mortgage broker isn't lying to you, you must think first about other things.

What if your car is getting old and will need to be replaced within a year? What if the house you're buying needs a new kitchen or bathroom that must be financed by a loan next year? Just two things alone that can cause significant hardship if you don't have borrowing power available beyond your mortgage payment. If you maximize all your borrowing power on your mortgage and its monthly principal and interest payments, you will not have room to borrow for another car, new or used. You won't have room to service a renovation loan for that kitchen or bathroom. You'll be what's referred to as being mortgage poor, meaning you can't afford to do anything, go anywhere or buy anything because all your money goes toward meeting your mortgage payment. How happy would you become in your larger, debt strapped home?

Your car may stop working, you won't be able to buy another and that could prevent you getting to work each day to earn a pay cheque to service your monthly commitments. See where we're going with this?

Plan two to five years down the road when applying for your mortgage. Consider the replacement of your car, loans you may need, and always the savings you would like to put away each month for your retirement. Do you have enough cash at the end of each month to contribute to an RRSP, an insurance product, or other investment? Have you considered that interest rates may rise significantly in the future compared to the rates you have now? If they do rise when you need to renew your mortgage it could be the difference between being able to afford your new big mortgage payment each month, and losing the home you have come to love, and worked so hard to acquire and make comfortable.

If you're going to ask someone to tell you how much of a mortgage you can afford, then ask them to also include a possible new loan and / or car payment that could happen within the next few years. They will look surprised with this request, but will include it into their debt servicing calculation. Don't be surprised that the amount of mortgage that was originally affordable, has likely been reduced by several thousands of dollars! This, realistically, is the amount of mortgage you should be considering as your maximum.

Try running different payment scenarios at higher interest rates to see if you're still able to afford that mortgage should the rates go up by the time you need to renew. Now, when something happens to that old car, or the house needs renovations, or rates go up significantly, you can proceed with confidence that you're able to afford the additional payments.

You may not have caught it yet, but you are managing a stronger credit rating through the above example. You know you can afford what you have, and can make increased payments should your circumstances change. No matter what, your credit rating will be preserved through all the changes that may come by, keeping your status as a preferred, healthy and strong client, with available borrowing power!

 It is easy to manage your own limits and credit rating. Don't leave it in the hands of people that may not always have your best interests in mind! It's your financial strength at stake; don't be so quick to hand it over.

NOTES

_____

_____

_____

_____

_____

_____

_____

_____

_____

_____

_____

_____

_____

_____

_____

_____

_____

_____

_____

_____

_____

_____

_____

NOTES

PART TWO

Understanding Banks
and
Financial Institutions

CHAPTER 13

What Kind of Business
Is A Bank In?

Aside from insurance, commodity and global market focuses, banks are in the business of lending money to retail and commercial markets to earn a profit. Profit (revenue) is earned through the collection of fees and interest.

The way it was

At one time local banks had the upper hand when it came time for their customers to borrow. Banks didn't try very hard to look for business; it kept walking in their front door. There was little competition around, and bank managers made the final decision on who would or would not be approved. Clients generally came dressed in their best clothes, with a well-rehearsed story to tell the bank manager why they needed a loan.

The way it is

With the launch of e-commerce and the age of Internet banking, customers are now able to shop from the comfort of their homes for the best rates, dressed however they wish. It is commonplace to complete applications on-line, never speaking with a person until documents need to be signed and information verified. Banks are changing their attitude to be more than customer focused; they have become aggressive opportunity-spotting specialists, ensuring the piece of your wallet they have remains theirs, and is given every opportunity to grow.

Their marketing strategies through call centres, target existing clients through retention activities such as financial advice. They hope to acquire more of your wallet while encouraging a stronger relationship with one bank, theirs. As you move more of your business to one bank they in turn offer lower lending rates, and higher rates of interest on your investments. Through this process you've become a preferred client in exchange for a larger share of your wallet.

Though helping to develop your credit rating will ultimately lead to more business for the bank, they are not particularly focused on giving out opportunities to help someone establish their credit. If you don't qualify, you'll need to bring a co-signer or co-borrower with you to make it work. Perhaps your credit is too damaged for even that, and if it is don't expect a bank to jump to your rescue. They are more interested in people with clean credit and are rated to be less risky to lend to as their payment history reflects continued good behaviour. That behaviour means they will be repaid and earn a profit, and that's just the kind of business the bank is in … being paid back to earn a profit.

Perhaps you drive a used car, or your job is new though secure. Maybe you've had a few credit problems in the past and are working hard to get ahead. Positioning your application for credit can make you look more desirable to become a client, than if you just spilled everything about your personal life. We'll talk about how to do this a little further on.

What do banks look for in a client?

Once bitten twice shy. If you failed to repay a loan to a creditor it's a safe bet that creditor will never lend to you again. The more creditors (lenders) you do this too, the more difficult it becomes to obtain credit from anyone. Be careful how many bridges you decide to burn. Not only will it appear on your credit bureau file, but also eventually no bank will lend to you! Its not just the banks you'll need to worry about then, but getting your phone hooked up without a significant deposit being requested, or a simple cell phone account will become an effort to activate.

Banks believe most people generally pay their bills on time and live their lives decently. Banks also realize they have to do a bang-up job to keep their preferred clients, or that business will travel elsewhere.

Remember what we said banks are looking for in a client? Clean credit, stable employment, regular income, and an address that doesn't change too often. In addition to these basics, a positive net worth and a growing savings account are a big plus when negotiating rates and security.

What's stable employment?

If your job is new but in the same industry there'll likely be no problem with your new employment tenure. For example: your prior job was a manager of a depart-ment store for two years and last year you crossed the street to the competition doing the same job. That's a total of three years income from the same industry.

If however, your job is new (less than one year) and in a different industry from your prior employment, borrowing may become a little more challenging. For example: you've secured a new job as a manager of a department store for the last six months, but were a cook at a fast food restaurant just prior, and unemployed prior to that for a lengthy period. Credibility plays a large roll in your life so watch out for those impulses that are risky endeavours.

CHAPTER 14

Think Like A Banker
To Be Properly Heard

Credit is a privilege, not a right. It is something that needs to be earned like respect. Don't expect to receive it without qualifying why you are eligible. Simply having a good story to tell does not advance your opportunity for success, or getting the lowest rate.

To understand how to get a good hearing by a lender, you need to understand what they are listening for when you make your case for a loan.

As you're telling your story why you need a loan, they're listening for particular comments around key areas of risk they need to satisfy. The risk is in lending to you, which considers your employment, address and marital stability (marital so far as if you have child support payments to make, or if you're splitting assets up that reduce your personal net worth), the amount of debt you carry, your net worth and your future plans or goals. Also, if you haven't heard it enough already, they are also listening for any indication as to the quality of your credit report before they spend the bank's money to purchase a copy for themselves.

So what does this mean to you? EVERYTHING!
The client interview is your first point of contact to begin

hearing their language, which I urge you to have it become yours. We'll call the language they speak, "*Sales Risk Assessment.*"

Have you heard the saying KISS? That is an acronym that means, "Keep It Simple Stupid," and to a borrower it means, "Say only what needs to be said."

Think through what you want to say before you push open their front door. It's impossible I agree, to plan an entire client interview without knowing the questions they'll ask you, but it's not impossible to be on your guard about what *not* to say.

Say as little as possible, and stick to the point. The loan officer will remember the conversation with you in point form anyway, so don't cloud their assessment with too many details and facts that are of interest to you that don't concern them. Stay away from telling lengthy stories about why you need the loan, "… my car broke down again and Christmas is around the corner! I really need this money to fix my car so I can go shopping." Just tell them the basic reason why you are sitting across from their desk, "I am applying for a loan to repair my car." Period.

They'll take quick notes on your employment history. Remember, it's not important how long you have been on the job but how long you've been in the industry. They're looking for stability. It is accepted that a large amount of people nowadays float from job to job due to contract employment, but they usually stay in the same field. The risk seen by the bank increases with lending to a person who moves from job to job while changing fields of focus. Increasing wage potential is a good reason to move but not always the best unless you can prove it.

Imagine you, as a carpenter, becoming a banker.

Wouldn't you like to see about three years stability before you determined that they succeeded in their career change? If they don't wait the three years, the person could lose their job, not get another because they don't know that market place well enough to work their network yet, and will likely switch to something else again. This sets up an unstable situation to a lender. This is not to say unique circumstances can be pigeonholed, if presented properly. Spend time determining your response to clearly communicate a unique situation, which does not cause a lender to assume employment stability is a negative trend for you.

Which one of these approaches do you think sounds better?

a) "I was fired from my last job because my manager didn't think I knew what I was doing! What a jerk, eh? Well, anyway, I left that place and found a new part time job through this temporary employment service. Good thing I was only unemployed for two weeks then or I would not of been able to make rent! I went to the cheque-cashing service for money, as the landlord would not take my cheque because they bounce sometimes. A few months later this new job really worked out well, they liked my work and offered me a full time position! It's only been about eight months but everything's going great for a change and I know I can meet the monthly payment for this new loan! I can even make the payment on my income alone if my wife decides to really leave me this time. Want to see my budget?"

b) "I have been working for my present employer for eight months. I passed my three month probationary period, am working full time hours and have had the same type of employment for the past seven years working for various companies in the same industry."

So when you're asked about your employment background use a KISS to keep it simple; let them know that you have been so many years in the same industry, currently working for ABC company earning a steady wage each year. Period. Don't start a conversation around how many times you've changed jobs unless asked, and then keep it brief. Never, never say anything like, "I had to leave that job 'cause my boss was a real idiot ... so I quit." Never knock anyone—especially yourself! Not a good opening line to build confidence that you will keep up your commitments. In bank language a comment like that would mean: *Doesn't like his boss, quits, couldn't like paying his loan each month, won't pay. Don't lend to this client.*

Make sure you have taken the time to thoroughly review your own credit report before the client interview, so you will be prepared to give a simple answer to any derogatory information. The lender may even pull your credit bureau file while sitting across from you, reading every line while they listen to see if you're disclosing everything. I would recommend giving them a copy of your credit report in advance to illustrate full disclosure, and add confidence to the lender with your state of readiness. When well prepared, you leave a lasting impression, because so many people are ill-prepared when walking into a bank's office!

It is truly refreshing for the lender to work with someone who has taken time to prepare before entering into the client interview. Lenders, at times, grow complacent when the client does the work in advance. There is a hidden benefit of being well prepared as the lender may quickly note the details for your application and send it on to their credit-granting department for final review, assuming for the most part that your information package was complete. With all the facts in front of the lender, who's focused on translating your situation and financial affairs into managing their risk to meet sales targets, they can help position your application for success. You will see this step alone saves you the greatest aggravation as fewer questions need to be asked, which means fewer answers need to be given, which means less negative perceptions are created. Failure normally follows a poorly presented application, which is a result of not telling the lender everything they need to know or by telling them too much!

 When you place in front of them a copy of your credit bureau report, attached to a list of your assets and your monthly liabilities (PSOA), your income verification (recent T4 slip, notice of assessment, recent pay stub and a letter from your employer if less than one year) and your open response to any negative credit items, their questions will be few.

Banks are focused on things they can prove. This means that if you have an arrangement with your ex-spouse to pay child support each month and it is not a legal agreement, there is no way a bank will know of this unless you offer the information. They also have no way of determining any private loans you may have outstanding to family members as these usually aren't noted legally either. So, again, keep it simple. But if they ask, tell the KISS truth.

When asked what liabilities you have, hand over your credit bureau report (the copy that you reviewed prior to making your loan appointment) and let them keep their records current to those items alone. These are the only items they can prove you are committed to repay, and you have already proven that the items on the report actually belong to you. They will pull their own copy to verify that yours has not been altered, isn't outdated, and is correct.

Banks are primarily concerned with items you legally must pay. If your child support or private loans aren't legally registered, you actually could stop paying them at any time by choice. Who's to say next month that the family member you owe money to won't forgive that loan altogether, or you paint their house or barter something else to repay them like trading your time to help them move? Maybe your parents will grant you an early gift of inheritance to help out? Or maybe you and your spouse reconcile differences to get back together only a month after your separation. If it's not a legal separation or divorce, it's a personal choice. If it's not on your credit bureau report, don't start talking about it unless the lender asks point blank, but then be positive about the situation! When and if that occurs, look at those circumstances accordingly while thinking through your response. It is prudent to go prepared. Preparation creates a perception of being complete and that you manage your affairs properly, and it is unlikely that surprise questions will be raised. When the lender can review all your affairs before asking a single question, they feel that much closer to completing the interview quickly and moving on to their next appointment—as should you.

When you've started a new job, and you're past the probationary period (usually three to six months), ask your employer to put in writing your date of hire, how much you're earning and the expected number of hours you will likely work in an average two week period and that they're pleased with your performance. This letter has a number of purposes that are of benefit to you.

Not only does it affirm you're in good standings with your employer, but it also establishes a starting wage for you in writing, as well as a commitment to the number of hours they expect you to work with them in a general pay period. It also becomes the tool you will need when you're applying for credit in the future, and it looks better when obtained before it is needed. Keep in mind most people don't receive an offer of employment from their employer before accepting their new job. This letter becomes a confirmation of employment for the individual, and is considered by a lender as a form of income verification. This letter along with a current pay stub, T4 slip and current notice of assessment is enough to prove your rate of income.

To your direct benefit as well, this letter becomes your proof that your new employer has to pay you that amount of wage or salary. It becomes your proof of engagement should there be a conflict with your pay cheques later on and you need to make an application through a government fairness board or adjudication committee for lost wages.

When speaking to a bank, keep in mind the few things shown below. They have sales targets just like any business. They have lending guidelines and rules to abide by. They have had bad experiences with some clients that have made them cautious, and the lender you will see during your appointment will likely have never met you before.

Sales targets are set by the bank for lenders to reach either by responding to people like you and I walking through their front door, or by calling us in the evenings. Their goals are also measurements of their productivity and are subject to review with their manager or supervisor. They *want* to sell you that loan, credit card or mortgage you're asking for. They *want* to position your application for an approval through their credit granting process and can't do that if you provide poor or inadequate information. If the lender can't get all the information needed to process your application, it may fall to the bottom of their to-do list until you follow up on your interview. Incompleteness prolongs your application, so be ready. Lenders need approvals as bad as you do, or they may not get a year-end sales bonus for reaching their targets. Give them what they need to help you, by being prepared.

This issue is set before you to provide a better appreciation for what drives a lender nowadays. Lenders have to prove they contribute to the bank's goals, or they are replaced with people who are more sales focused. Knowing this, it is safe to say that they want you to get that loan too, and will try as hard as they can to get it approved without knowingly making up a lie about you or defrauding the bank. When you come prepared with your credit information in hand, employment letter(s), income and employment verification you're more likely not to be questioned about things as the lender has the necessary information required to complete their application. Problems start when the lender asks a simple question and the client goes into a detailed or long-winded answer, often telling the lender more than they need to know, closing doors on their application.

If you volunteer that you and your spouse have agreed to live apart for a period of time, questions arise about issues of potential child support payments, assets being sold off to pay out a spouse, as well as the risk that either spouse could charge every joint family card to their maximum limits buying for themselves before finally committing to a legal divorce. Remember, its nobody's business that your marriage or common-law relationship is going through a tough time, and who's to say that you both won't work it out once a little time has passed?

A legal divorce is final, and usually a lender will have a question on your marital status. I prefer to think you are either married, or single. It's nobody's business if you're divorced. After all, a divorce document legally declares you're single from that individual. If you signed an agreement that you are to pay child support as a condition to the divorce/separation, it will show on your credit bureau so it's wise to disclose in advance your changed marital status. Don't give details on any assets that may be sold. Stick to the facts (KISS) by describing only what is legally binding. If your divorce agreement states that the marital home is to be sold, be prepared to discuss the details of the legal agreement. Will one spouse buy the other out? Is the property expected to be listed through a realtor? If there is a mortgage against the house, you will be asked about the details. If you own it free and clear, you also may want to share this to entice the lender that you will be coming into substantial cash from the equity once the house sells. The lenders begin to think you will bring that cash to them as a deposit (GIC, RRSP, etc.) and help them reach their sales targets. Remember, they will probably ask to see a copy of the final divorce/separation agreement to verify all that you've just related. If you start telling stories that are untruthful or which can't make clear sense, the lender will be more diligent in the client interview to ensure you're telling the truth about everything. Don't raise yellow flags! Stick to the facts, and don't make up stories as you go along!

Keep in mind they are not making personal decisions for or against you. They are making risk decisions. What is the risk in lending to you that the bank won't be repaid? That is the primary question they're answering throughout your application. The information they request from you is put through a language filter, translating what you say into risk for the adjudicators who will review your stated information to understand the lenders recommendation to support you. The adjudicators either agree or disagree with how the lender has determined how acceptable the risk is in lending to you.

 Don't sign anything you haven't read or completely understand. If a lender explains something you're unsure of, get them to write it out, sign and date it, so you'll have proof of the conversation should they be wrong.

CHAPTER 15

Meet Mrs. Robinson

Mrs. Robinson, a fictional character, is applying for a loan when a lender asks her, "What loans and credit cards do you currently have?"

Mrs. Robinson replies, "Here's a recent copy of my credit bureau report I received last week. Can you tell from this what you need?"

The lender, relieved that Mrs. Robinson came prepared with a recent credit report, will key into the application all the trade lines on that report. They will still pull their own credit report on Mrs. Robinson to cross check the information, likely not asking her that same question again.

Mrs. Robinson didn't outline with the lender all her liabilities one by one. She answered the question with a question, which the lender accepted as an answer. She didn't get into any conversations about why she has a *private* loan with her mother. The lender received the necessary information they required to process the application, confirmed all liabilities against the credit bureau report and is now closer to meeting sales targets and finishing this appointment with Mrs. Robinson.

Mrs. Robinson had also lent $30,000 to her sister, and

has not shown that loan as an asset nor as a monthly income, as it can't be proven.

On the credit report Mrs. Robinson provided there were no overdrafts on any of her chequing or savings accounts, no outstanding mortgages or pending divorce discussions, no cable or telephone repayment histories, or the fact that she owes her mother $20,000. Nobody can tell that the loan her mother gave her was for the new car she drives as her credit bureau would show if she had a loan with another bank for that new car, or if it were a lease through a dealer. Private money (loan or investment) isn't tracked and can't be disputed without evidence. In essence, private loans are invisible. She was asked if she owned or rented the property put down as her mailing address. Mrs. Robinson, not trying to elude the lender about her mortgage with the bank down the street, willingly shared she does in fact own the property and has a small mortgage against it even though her credit bureau report does not show a mortgage on it.

Keep in mind there will be a question somewhere throughout the application process that she will need to answer in writing (sign to) confirming that she has disclosed all the facts and has not knowingly withheld pertinent information that could impact the bank's decision. Mrs. Robinson feels the interpretation of the word facts is open for discussion. She perceives only legal items as facts, not the repayment of family loans.

Mrs. Robinson still has a commitment to repay her mother each month though the terms frequently change, even to the point of skipping numerous payments. This type of commitment is difficult to explain, even that her mother has agreed that when she doesn't have ready cash that she doesn't need to pay that month. Mrs. Robinson did not sign a note with her mother promising to repay her. There is little legal standing about this family loan, other than a mutual understanding. If it ever became complicated, her mother would have a difficult time trying to sue or prove her daughter owes her. Mrs. Robinson actually repays the loan to her mother from the monthly payment her sister gives her on her loan, not using her own cash to pay back her mother.

A bank's loan is very legal and must be repaid as you signed a loan note committing your promise to repay. It's easier to ask Mom and Dad to wait an extra month for that payment, or to reduce the payment amount, than it is to ask a bank to do the same without raising yellow flags.

Good thing Mrs. Robinson came prepared! The entire process took twenty minutes to complete from the time Mrs. Robinson entered the lender's office to leaving the bank. She will have her answer within twenty-four hours, and likely will be approved.

When a person walks into a bank branch, and meets with a lender to tell their story of woe, they will receive no money on that reason alone. Though the story may be very real and life altering, it isn't enough to get a loan nowadays. All the words and paper can't deter that it all comes down to how much cash you have each month to service your commitments, and the strength of your credit report.

Banks do care about what you want the loan for, but there isn't a huge emphasis placed on it. It is best to keep your reason for needing the loan as a simple one, like investment reasons, or small home repairs. If you are applying for a loan to refinance or consolidate all your existing debt to minimize your monthly payments you may be declined for that reason alone.

Refinancing your affairs is viewed as a yellow flag, and may indicate that you're having credit trouble or cash flow problems that are beyond your ability to fix. Though a refinance loan makes sense in a lot of cases, less monthly payments, less interest etc., it makes lenders uneasy. It's unlikely that you will be successful convincing a lender your refinancing situation is not a risk, even though in most cases refinancing or consolidating debt is a good idea. If you continue to apply for a refinance or consolidation loan, you may be forced to sit across the desk of a high-risk lender. These lenders will lend to you, and charge a premium to do it. These types of loans take longer to repay due to more of the monthly payments being spent on interest, rather than reducing the principal. Put aside your desperation, as you need to review your needs and how much debt you have to refinance before approaching this type of lender. You're at the end of the road, using a lender of last resort.

An *investment loan* needs to be very broad by description. It can be used for anything that generates a return on principal. Consolidating debt can be viewed as a wise investment strategy, minimizing interest thereby generating savings on your debt instrument. This can also be positioned as a return on your investment. The investment being the new loan to pay out all the other loans and save money using lower monthly payments. It's all in the personal interpretation of what exactly the word "investment" means to you.

Speaking "bank" usually means you've clearly presented your current debt commitments, proof of income, and employment stability to a lender that is now able to take that information, key it into an electronic application and send it to their credit granter without too much difficulty ascertaining the risk they will take in lending to you. Keep it clear, clean and simple.

That's it.

 Prepare all your questions ahead of time when you want to ask about loan terms, amortizations and rates. This will help to keep you focused during the client interview, and will keep the lender on their toes to offer you choices. Leave space between your questions to add notes that you can review later.

NOTES

_____

_____

_____

_____

_____

_____

_____

_____

_____

_____

_____

_____

_____

_____

_____

_____

_____

_____

_____

_____

_____

_____

NOTES

_____

_____

_____

_____

_____

_____

_____

_____

_____

_____

_____

_____

_____

_____

_____

_____

_____

_____

_____

_____

_____

_____

_____

_____

_____

PART THREE

The Retail Lending Process

Minimize Numerous Banking Applications

Apply once, with one Banker

The days are gone when we could walk into a bank and speak with the manager, who knew us since our parents set up our first savings account. Knowing who the bank manager is nowadays carries with it little weight. Bank managers are now sales managers, focused on building teams to book business. Most financial institution's focus has changed and no longer carries the personal attention that is found woven through their historical foundation. The branch manager now co-ordinates staff and targets marketing sales efforts. When going to your branch to apply for credit, you begin a process that will whisk you away faster than you'll anticipate. The process for applying is swift, as are the decisions. Reversing decisions and adding new information (amendments) to your application after the adjudication (decision) process is difficult and annoying at times because it's streamlined to review applications, not amendments to them. You will likely not be able to speak with the adjudicator about the details of your application either. Everything you need to communicate needs to be explained to a bank representative and they in turn rephrase what you have said and forward the details on to their adjudicator. (Review Part 2— Chapter 13, 14, 15 Understanding Banks)

Centralized adjudicators are busy reviewing credit requests from across the country so their time is highly valuable and in great demand. To keep reviewing the same application with numerous amendments is annoying, and they are likely to post a standing decline to your application just so they can move on. This is another solid reason why presenting your application as complete as possible the first time is so important. Don't rely on the local bank officer to simply grant you a loan.

Often people believe that it matters what branch they apply to will make a difference to being approved. In today's networking environment, the first banker contacted enters your application(s). A separate team, likely in another city, reviews your credit application that was received electronically through a web-based or e-mail type process, and responds back to the banker on whether the application for credit has been approved or declined. The banker in turn informs you, the applicant, of their decision. Going to another branch of the same bank to apply for the same loan does little good. If they take an application from you it could be simply to humour you. They know the same lending review team that declined your previous application will review it again with the same result if nothing major has changed. Also, the second banker will be noted for submitting a duplicate application for the same loan that was shown as refused on the computer. Most bankers will not submit a second application on your behalf, rather referring you to the original banker to review your options.

It's important to be reminded that when something important was not mentioned or realized in your first application, then let the first banker know and ask for an amendment to be considered. This shows that your intentions are to add clarity to your first application rather than take what you learned from the process and try again with another banker, perhaps altering your information in a way to misrepresent the facts in your determination to get your loan. If a note shows on their computer system that they suspect this is happening, your chances of obtaining credit now or in the future becomes very compromised. A bank's database has a long memory, so keep the information on a bank's database as clear and truthful as possible!

If your bank declines your application, make an effort to understand why. Learn from it. Don't just throw your hands in the air, march off down the street in a huff and do the same thing at the next bank. If you do, don't be surprised when they also decline you. You're not just asking for a loan, you're asking the bank to start building a relationship with you. That's something they don't have to do if you don't fit their criteria as a good risk. They don't have to grant a loan to you just because you qualify.

Once you understand the reasons surrounding your declined application, make the necessary changes before re-applying. Review your credit bureau report for errors. Go over options with the lender that took your initial application to ensure they have all the correct information. If you're unclear ask to speak to another lender, someone to review the application with a fresh set of eyes, perhaps someone with more lending experience. Sometimes a more knowledgeable lender can work with a declined application and turn it into an approval by presenting your information differently (presentation is everything) and that's why it's so important to understand what they are listening for when interviewing you so you can present your affairs in a way with which they can work with. We will review more about this in the next section.

If after listening and working with your bank, your application is still declined and you feel it should be approved, take what you have learned and try applying at another bank. Perhaps your bank will refer another to you they know that may be tolerant to your particular decline reasons. Financial institutions, which lend to higher risk applicants, also charge more due to the risk there is in that you may not repay them.

What is "tied selling?"

"We will approve your new loan only if you move all your investments, mortgage and credit card business to us first."

You have just had your arm twisted by someone applying a lender's technique called "tied-selling." This is illegal, and means that you are being pressured to bring other business to that lending institution as a condition of your approval. I would recommend calling the Ombudsman's office (Review Chapter 2—Myths on Borrowing: List of Ombudsman offices) if you suspect this type of behaviour is happening. Tied-selling amongst sales staff is not tolerated by financial institutions or the law, and appropriate action will be taken if in fact tied-selling is happening.

Section 459.1 of the Bank Act prohibits banks from practicing coercive tied selling. As stated in the act it is specifically against the law for a bank to "impose undue pressure on, or coerce, a person to obtain a product or service from a particular person, including the bank and any of its affiliates, as a condition for obtaining another product or service from the bank."

Don't confuse tied-selling with necessary security required to secure a loan, and the comfort levels a bank may not have around putting a collateral mortgage on your property which is financed through another bank. Ask for clarity if this issue comes up to ensure tied-selling is not what's happening. Ask the question, "Is this tied-selling?" and listen closely to their response. Ask to see the manager, and advise you would like to contact their Ombudsman's office immediately if it appears to be a genuine tied-selling approach.

 Though it is illegal for a bank to tie-sell a loan approval, it isn't illegal for you to offer to move all your business to that financial institution to entice them to approve your loan. This type of leverage could be a strategy to your advantage, as you hold out a carrot for them to nibble on.

The Financial Consumer Agency of Canada (FCAC) supervises all federally-regulated financial institutions to ensure that they comply with federal consumer protection provisions. These provisions encapsulate a variety of operating practices that directly effect customers of financial institutions.

You're able to call the FCAC for more information on regulatory issues they govern by dialling 1-866-461-3222. If you have a regulatory complaint it will be reviewed on a case-by-case basis, and should be addressed in writing to:

FINANCIAL CONSUMER AGENCY OF CANADA (FCAC)
6th Floor, Enterprise Building
427 Laurier Ave., West
Ottawa, Ontario
K1R 1B9

The electronic application

With technology as advanced as it is today, we should touch on the fact that banks keep detailed profiles on each client. The quality of the profile information depends on the type of internal computer infrastructure that exists for that bank. Most banks in Canada have a global presence, and a strong computer network infrastructure. This also means that they likely have a detailed history of all the applications you've made to them for credit over the years, along with each lender notes and comments electronically saved and accessible to any employee of that bank, in any branch around the world.

Though your bank has a file for you, it is not accessible by competitive banks or financial lending institutions. No bank can provide or discuss your personal affairs with another bank. In fact, they can't say anything to another client about your affairs, and if they do they are in violation of your right to client privacy like a lawyer/client and could be sued for doing so. They can put a collection claim on your credit bureau report to tip off other would-be lenders when you're not being or acting responsible, but they can't call other banks to tell them they are having a bad experience with you and your loan payments.

Let's look at your file at your primary bank.

This file has a detailed history of each application you have made in the past for credit through them. It may surprise you to learn that the first loan you applied for is still on file, even if it was declined. Each mortgage application declined or approved is shown. Each refinance application, if you've refinanced your home before, and each credit card application you've completed at your bank is also on record.

The electronic application was developed to not only provide lenders with a historic picture for each client, but to centralize the approval and information process while moving more toward a paperless environment and a centralized records management system. Whether you call the bank's 1-800 number, walk into a branch or access their internet web site to complete an application, they all are saved the same way, and are routed to the same credit-granting department. This is to say that it doesn't matter what medium you chose to apply, the same people review your application for credit in most preferred banks.

Let's assume that you've called the telephone application centre's 1-800 number. You've answered all their questions, and while you're on the phone they softly decline you by saying, "Your application for credit has been declined for the following reason: low income, low net worth, poor credit, etc." You feel that the person on the phone hasn't taken you application fairly, or doesn't understand something you're trying to explain that may change things. They will likely refer you to speak to your home branch and to make a personal appointment with a lender.

There are a few reasons a call centre may say this to you. They are measured each day on the amount of applications they can complete over the phone, how many actually get approved, and how long it takes them to complete each application. If the call centre phone representative begins to suspect that they won't be able to make your application work quickly, they will abandon their efforts and refer you to your branch to work it out. You hang up, and they go to their next caller in their search to complete another application.

When you visit your home branch and its lender, they can electronically access, to review the application you completed over the phone, and can quickly review the notes the call centre representative made to help them identify the weaknesses of the application. They will be able to make their own assessment to the facts, capture from your client interview new or missing details and re-submit your application to the same credit-granting group that reviewed your application the first time. The only difference between going into a branch to complete your application, and doing it over the phone is that you are right across the desk of the person trying to help you. You're connected in a far different way and able to communicate using your tone in your voice, body language, eyes, and facial expression. You can address head-on any issue the lender may need to overcome to make your application work, and you feel a sense of community with your bank while going through the process that a telephone representative or Internet platform application can't sustain.

It is easier to lobby for support when you're visible; the lender is more likely to help position your information favourably because you're sitting right there in front of them. They can evaluate what your presence and actions mean. They also can prepare an amendment to the application the phone representative completed in the first place.

Now don't be misled! The lender sitting across from you has goals to meet and sales targets too, and isn't likely to beat an application again and again if they know that it won't work. Another reason why it is so important to come prepared (and I recommend actually completing the application at a branch, not a call centre) so the lender can submit a solid, clear and simple application to their credit granting department the first time. This avoids credit departments asking the lender, "Why is this client applying on the phone, faxing a paper application and now seeing you in person? Don't they know we're going to decline them again?"

If you like rules to live by, then these are the rules to use when seeking a loan so your chances of being approved are better;

i)   Never rush into borrowing and signing papers.
ii) Make your first effort the best.
iii) Be prepared and know your financial readiness before applying.
iv) Have a firm handle on your debts and repayment history information.

Alternate delivery applications

What sometimes doesn't show on your file is an application for a credit card through an alternate delivery process. Alternate delivery is a paper-based application you've picked up through a brochure your bank puts out that you fax to a centralized location for processing. Sometimes a mail out pre-approval application is sent to your home address by your financial institution that you've been accepted. As you did not complete the application in person in a branch, it is likely the only evidence they have is the paper copy of your manual application form. Though these are reduced and stored on a piece of film, they are not electronically accessible by any lender in any city. They would need to order a copy of this information from their records management department and wait a few days for a copy to arrive. As this adds little value while completing your new credit application, and takes time to request, lenders don't usually require this historical information. Having said all that, they do review your prior applications for credit while completing your new application. This allows them to see if your job stability is all you say it is, along with your income levels, marital status and current address.

Does your bank know too much?

Is it possible for your bank to know too much about you, given they have had you for a long time as their client? Consider for the moment that you walked down the street to the other bank, completed their application with the same information as your bank has, and were approved. How could this happen? Let's look at Mrs. Robinson again.

It turns out that Mrs. Robinson quit her job the previous month, and when she was asked to provide her T-4 income slip with her notice of assessment the lender assumed she was still employed. After all, Mrs. Robinson came prepared with a copy of her credit bureau report from both bureaus, all her income verification and knew the rates of loans currently being offered. She was well prepared, and it was assumed she was still working with the same company. Mrs. Robinson had since accepted a new job with a different company doing the same thing as before, and was confident she would be able to pay for the new loan before she decided to apply. The lender at this financial institution didn't ask any further questions about her emplyment stability (which they should have) and processed her application. Mrs. Robinson would have answered the KISS truth had the lender required more information about her employment, and perhaps been required at that time to provide additional information regarding her new job.

Well, the lender at her bank had known her for 15 years, and also knew the manager of the company Mrs. Robinson worked for. While out on a business lunch the manager of the company mentioned to that lender that Mrs. Robinson just quit one day, and never came back. With that extra bit of privileged information, the bank manager declined to process Mrs. Robinson's application thinking she was unemployed. The bank manager didn't know she had a new job, and that her probationary period was over in two months. The bank down the street didn't know Mrs. Robinson or her employer, and were not aware of the same privileged information, and therefore it was not used in their assessment of the risk in lending to her. They took her application, keyed in the information they extracted from Mrs. Robinson's prepared information package and positioned it for an approval.

CHAPTER 17

How To Use
The Centralized Application

Not too many years ago an appointment with the branch manager would be needed to discuss your loan. You'd sit down and explain your situation. The manager (hopefully you want them to be an ally) would consider your request, complete a few documents and you would often have the funds in your account before you left. If the bank manager didn't like you, or had a negative perception about you or your situation you probably would find yourself on the street still looking for the loan.

Banks have taken major strides to bridge this gap over the past ten years. They have diversity-focused mandates to eliminate prejudicial lending decisions, and centralized adjudication to further displace the decision maker from the client to help eliminate these types of conclusions. Most banks are in a marathon to brand themselves as trustworthy advisors, ready to serve you as quickly as possible without compromising your privacy. They truly want to replace the slogan "It's who you know," with, "It's what bank you know." They prefer to be identified as a lean machine with a great team rather than a few good people working for a company who genuinely want to help you.

Because of this focus, coupled with consideration to serve their clients more efficiently and cost effectively, the centralized adjudication process was developed and continues to be fine tuned as the times evolve. There are a few facts we need to accept when applying for money in this modern age of lending:

1) It doesn't matter what branch where you apply. Most of the big banks have their branches send loan applications to the same place for review and approvals. If you don't like the decision the first branch gave you and you think you'll go to another one of your bank's branches to re-apply successfully, you're mistaken. The second application would be routed through the same adjudication process; possibly even to the same adjudicator who would have concerns as to why you are reapplying with another branch. You are able to, however, apply at a completely different bank with a fresh start, as they may not have a file on you. (Please review Part 3—Chapter 16, The Electronic Application.)

2) Going prepared means you have a better understanding of your own needs, and how to best present them to a bank. Lenders value a prepared applicant as it saves them time, gives them greater credibility and they will find they're in a position to represent your needs clearly to their centralized adjudicator. (Please review Part 2—Chapter 4, Think Like A Banker To Be Properly Heard.)

3) Because centralized adjudication exists, built around an electronic application delivery process,

heavy emphasis is placed on the results of your credit bureau report. It should be your priority to review all the reports available on you, and confirm the information is in fact about you, and is accurate *before* you apply for a loan. (Please review Part 1—Chapter 7, Understanding Your Credit Bureau).

Now that we accept banking isn't as much about *who you know* as it is *what they know about you* that influences the approval process, let's consider for a moment that we have a greater influence now than we ever have before over the information they review to determine approvals. We have discovered that debt servicing and our credit bureaus pretty much account for the majority of their decision. If we have the cash available to service the monthly loan payments, and we're not exceeding the TDS and GDS ratios (Please review Part 1—Chapter 5, Debt Servicing) we're almost there! All we have to do is ensure our repayment history with other creditors is consistently satisfactory, or have a good reason as to why it fails the test.

If nothing else, remember this

Remember one simple fact over all others: Your credit bureau report is a reflection of your payments habits. It is this financial fingerprint that can't be rubbed out just with wishful thinking! Keep your credit profile information current, accurate and clean of any negative at all times.

Use only enough credit to service your needs, no more. Stay away from applying for cards or credit you don't need, and regularly review your credit report at least once a year to ensure it remains accurate and up to date each year. This is a must do before you apply for a loan. This practice of continually maintaining the perception of how you are seen is in your direct control as is the information contained on your report. Your credit bureau report provides a lot of the credit decision for your application, and could be the strongest influence affecting your success or failure.

What's a Scoring Model?

Though a "Scoring Model" isn't made of oil or water-colours, it does paint a picture!

Once your information has been entered into the application and sent to the centralized adjudicators it will pass through a risk filter. This filter measures the likelihood the lender will be repaid over the term of the loan, and if the risk is acceptable. How is this measured you may ask? Well, this is where we concentrate on the scoring model.

A scoring model is like a comparison, where the information gathered in your application is measured against a database of collected information and repayment risk scenarios, predetermining the likelihood you will repay your loan based on the experience the bank has had in the past with applications similar to yours. Consider over the years all the applications a bank has reviewed, all the information available to them to determine the profile of a potential delinquent loan, and how to identify its many factors *before* lending! Often, a bank will purchase the scoring model that has been developed from historical information. The scoring model does not in itself compare your application one at a time with the millions before yours, it merely measures yours against a series of ranges that are unique to applications that have proven to be desirable for repayment.

Most scoring models have a credit bureau component built into them, automatically pulling in a recent report to the scoring model scenario to measure your financial fingerprint, that all-important repayment history. You may have a strong cash flow to service the new loan, but your credit report says you're a slow payer, or loans have been written off in the past because you refuse to pay. To make a proper risk assessment when lending, the model considers your historical repayment habits from your credit report, similar applications like yours from the past, to determine the likelihood of being repaid. Your current employment details, salary, additional income and its strength, co-signers/borrowers, asset values and much, much, more are all weighed against scoring models identified as being of acceptable risk. There could be over 100 key points that are measured through a scoring model to determine the degree of risk with lending to a particular applicant. There could also be as few as four points measured depending on the amount of credit you are applying for at the time, and through what financial institution.

Scoring models don't just measure the type of information presented, they also measure *how* you've entered it. For example, let's say that Mrs. Robinson was completing an application at her department store for a credit card. She decides that she doesn't want to enter how much salary she earns a year and leaves it blank. The scoring model may view the type of person that leaves a blank for that question usually pays their bills on time, and simply takes exception to sharing how much income they earn. It could also view the blank negatively. These assumptions, being true or false, contribute to the overall application score.

All scoring models are different in some way, and change often. Be careful, stay alert, and stay on track.

The financial institutions scoring model is likely to give a bonus point or two if you're already a customer of the financial institution you're applying to. If you do all your banking with them they can easily determine how strong a customer you have been. Have you repaid your loans in the past to them? Are all your credit cards with them up to date? Do you have a chequing or savings account set up for your day-to-day banking needs? If you answer "Yes" to these questions, the financial institution will prefer to lend to you as an existing client than to a new client where they have no first hand experience. Having said this, your application still passes through the scoring model filter, but with the strength of an existing customer.

 Sometimes it is advantageous to have an account with two major banks, to provide the opportunity to apply as an existing customer with both if one declines you. Swing your loyalty as your needs and their products change.

Department store credit cards likely never make it past the scoring model stage. Your application is either accepted or declined and there is no way to go back to try to get your application re-scored. In fact, you probably won't be able to speak with someone regarding your application. Think twice before applying for this type of credit. At least through a bank you're able to appeal the decision at least once by speaking with a person who can help reposition your application depending on what needs to be improved.

When applying through a bank, the experience of the person completing your application may also impact the credit decision. Positioning and wording is everything. An experienced lender has foresight in knowing how to word your information in a way that may appear more reasonable than a newer lender who has less experience assessing risk. This is a small influence in the overall scoring model process, but still is an influence. Find out the number of years of experience the lender has before you firm up your appointment. Try to speak with a lender who has been working with credit applications for a few years, someone also experienced in mortgages. This individual will likely have a refined foresight to further assist with positioning your application for success. After all, just presenting the facts isn't everything; it's how you present them that counts when the wire is tight! Selecting an experienced interviewer for the client interview is also important. Though you may feel that you have no choice of who interviews you to review your application, sometimes you're able to request a particular person to conduct the interview. Do a little homework at your branch to understand who's the most experienced lender, and try to request that they meet with you.

CHAPTER 18

Moving On From Prior Bankruptcy

The answer may be "No" now, but that's not a "No" forever!

If you're about two years from your bankruptcy discharge and have re-established at least one new form of credit (department store credit card, etc.,) you may have a chance of being approved for a loan or mortgage. Typically though lenders are looking to see that your bankruptcy discharge was at least three years prior to applying with at least two years established credit. If you experienced a foreclosure or power of sale you may not qualify for housing insurance on your next real-estate purchase.

Sometimes the reason you went bankrupt can also make a difference. Was it due to a divorce, or business partnership failure? There are some justifiable reasons why people declare bankruptcy other than just not paying their bills. Though most financial institutions are leery when reviewing prior bankruptcy applications, they are open to listening to how you have worked to re-establish yourself.

The easiest way to improve your credit rating is to secure a loan through a loan broker or high-risk lender. They will charge you a high interest rate, but that's the price for re-establishing your credit. Repay the loan as fast as possible. Make sure they report your repayment history to the credit bureau or you are not clearly re-establishing your credit rating. Try to apply with various department stores for a low limit credit card, or buy a piece of furniture on a don't-pay-for-a-year promotion. Pay it off before the year is up.

Though these are easy steps to re-establish your credit rating, it will take time to see it through. Be patient. You are starting over, like a student fresh out of school looking for their first car loan. You may need a co-signer or co-borrower to make it happen. If so, only apply for a small amount, repay the loan quickly and then try to apply for another on your own strength.

You may need to obtain several loans with co-signers and repay them all to re-establish your credit. After doing this a few times, it will be easier for a bank scoring model to identify that you have re-established your credit, even though it is lower than you once had.

You may find that if you included a bank as a creditor in your bankruptcy, that they may never want to lend to you again. Once bitten, twice shy. It may be wise to simply move on from that bank and find another willing to start over with you.

Are you self-employed?

(Please review Part 1—Chapter 10, Your Income And How You Report It)

When self-employed and applying for a loan, there are extra matters for you to attend to. You will likely have to prove a three-year income average, and possibly provide year-end financial statements for your limited company, if you have a name that is registered with a provincial government or federally. Usually a credit rating on the company is not considered as part of your application, but if you're a sole owner your personal credit rating is the same as your company because all your personal and business debt is in your personal name already.

If your loan is for a limited company or partnership, have the business apply on its own strength. The company's accountant-prepared financial statement is the necessary tool a lender requires to review any "add-back" items to help increase the amount of cash the company has available to service debt after all its commitments are met. If the business can't support the debt, be cautious that the loan or mortgage you're applying for is the right decision for you and how it affects you personally. At the end of the day whether the business can repay the loan or not, you're totally responsible to repay it if you're personally guaranteeing the debt, or taking it out in your name to invest it in the company.

The borrowing process isn't much different for self-employed as it is for others. You complete the same application, only your income is more difficult to substantiate.

 Be *very* certain you want to structure the debt for a business in your personal name.

CHAPTER 19

Assure Privacy and Security of Your Personal Information

A hot point of conversation today without doubt, is how secure people feel (and are) with their personal information being shared on the Internet.

How secure they feel, and how secure they are, I believe are two completely different matters. Feelings don't necessarily trace back to facts. They are feelings. You feel hot. You feel cold. You feel secure. These feelings don't illustrate awareness that everybody is hot, cold, or secure.

Feelings are personal, and go toward shaping our perceptions and opinions on the environments we find ourselves strolling through on a daily bases. I believe, in part, our feelings actually dictate what type of security measures we need to put in place, to develop our personal sense of security, to ensure if you will, that we feel secure. Sometimes this means, unfortunately, that we stick our heads in the sand to save our feelings or we are left searching in the dark for something to hold onto so we don't feel stranded (hopefully we are not holding on to the handle that triggers the trap door we are standing on). Often, perhaps without reason, we take estranged comfort when somebody else tells us we are safe and not to worry about our discomfort.

Understanding what privacy and security means may go a long way to understanding if your personal information, is in fact, secure. Try purchasing a book that talks about security issues on the Internet to get the real story. Find out for yourself what's secure, and what isn't. Take time to understand what encryption is all about, and the differences between phone and cable Internet service provides (from a security perspective) if you're a frequent Internet shopper.

Less than twenty years ago, the postal service was the major security blanket we grew to trust as they handled most of our personal security information in the form of letters, documents and parcels. We could measure quite easily if something was missing, because it usually was the only way we would send or receive personal or confidential items.

Postal security is good for the most part over what they can control. There still is little protection against the person hiding in the bushes waiting to lift the letters from your mailbox. Your personal information remains at risk as long as it takes you to pick up your mail.

 If your outside mailbox is unattended for long periods of time, try opening a post office mailbox that can be monitored for a small monthly fee. This increases your control over securing personal information found in many items you receive by mail. That P.O. box becomes a monitored security system!

Today, with a steady flurry of commerce flowing back and forth the world's borders are blurring more than ever. Different time zones don't appear to affect a transaction closing in real global time, which really is no time at all. I won't be surprised the day we accept the concept of a global standard time, in it's natural progression toward standardization of the commerce sales cycle and how the people who measure these things get a handle of just how many dollars are flowing back and forth, and to where and when.

The question, again, is how secure are we in the middle of this continually evolving, refining, and uniting infrastructure we have come to accept as the internet?

Today we have no solid way to police or monitor all the traffic, or kind of traffic, that travels on the web. With the telecommunications financial fall of 2001, we witnessed from their balance sheets just how many dollars went into creating this immense resource. It will not go away, it has only stalled mid-flight while the market catches up to the infrastructure that awaits its command. Individuals and companies are in the processes now of redefining their communication needs to maximize this resource's capability.

So here we are, in the transition state of privacy and security of the companies that hold our personal information in a digital file or database, fumbling to understand how to protect it to earn our trust. Though their intentions remain constant with keeping our personal information safe, they are learning to adapt. Criminals, sadly, are learning to manipulate their security measures as fast as they are implemented it seems.

Peter Waldie published an article in *The Globe and Mail* Wednesday, February 19, 2003, titled, "FBI investigates massive breach of credit card security." In it he says, "The FBI is investigating how a hacker accessed account numbers of about eight million credit card holders in North America, including at least 100,000 Canadians. Experts said it is unclear what information may have been taken, but noted it is the largest credit card security breach ever."

In the same article Mr. Waldie quotes Rosaleen Citron, CEO of White-Hat Inc. (a Burlington, Ontario-based information technology security company) as saying, "Somebody got in there and whether it came from the inside or the outside, it was a breach. Generally people don't do this unless they are looking for something, usually monetary gain."

Mr. Waldie goes on to report that MasterCard said about 2.2 million of its account numbers were "possibly compromised," including 40,000 in Canada. Visa said about 3.4 million account numbers "have the potential to have been compromised," including 60,000 in Canada. American Express and Morgan Stanley officials did not comment on the number of accounts affected.

The hacker managed to break into the database of a U.S. company that processes credit card transactions for merchants. In Canada, credit card transactions are generally processed through banks, but in the United States dozens of companies provide the service.

Mr. Peter Hope-Tindall (security consultant at Mississauga, Ontario-based Data Privacy Partners Ltd.) was quoted in the same article as saying, "We haven't seen anything of this magnitude. It's the uncertainty that's the killer." Mr. Hope-Tindall went on to explain, "New anti-fraud measures have prompted many American companies to require some personal information from customers buying items with credit cards."

Less than a week earlier, Jane Gadd (court reporter) published an article also found in The Globe and Mail on Thursday, February 13, 2003 reporting a Russian organized-crime gang was uncovered operating in Vancouver Canada working a banking-machine fraud scheme. The $1.2-million scheme involved their purchasing and distributing banking machines, which were rigged to download users' bankcard numbers and personal identification codes into computers operated by gang members. Duplicate bankcards were then produced and used to withdraw cash. The unsettling part for me is in how this scheme was discovered. The article describes that one gang member was ejected from a car in a dispute with another. She made her way to Toronto, where she was arrested at Union Station along with bags and boxes containing bundles of $20.00 bills. The five Canadian banks hit with the fraudulent withdrawals absorbed the losses for their customers.

These types of fraud and many others are taking us silently by storm. Our personal information is being stolen, copied and reproduced as easily as the two above articles have described. (Please review: Part 1, Chapter 7—Identity Theft).

How secure is your personal information with financial institutions? As secure as it can be, I suppose.

My mother taught me to not tell anybody anything I didn't want broadcast over the school P.A. system when I was growing up. It's good advice to pass along when you want to keep a secret. Really what she was saying was that I better know exactly whom I'm telling my secret to, and that they truly are my friend before sharing. If we use these same words of caution for our personal information, we are doing the best job we can toward securing our identities.

Don't share your personal information with anybody you truly don't know anything about. This includes completing information forms for contest, draws for prizes or other medias that require you first to complete a personal information section before they will give you something. If you like contests and prizes, buy a dollar lottery ticket.

Think twice before filling in personal information on a web page. Put aside for a moment that the page clearly advises they are secure, and to trust them. Determine your sense of security on your own. Do you truly know what this business is all about? Do you know where their physical location is, or are they an "invisible" merchant? Is there a risk they will sell your information to another company, or another person without your knowledge? Would you have any recourse if they did do this? Would you ever be able to prove they sold your information? Is it possible a hacker could sneak into their data storage facilities and steal all their clients personal files, including yours? These questions can go on and on, and they should in your own mind. As *The Globe and Mail* articles illustrate, it doesn't matter how hard financial institutions try to protect your personal information, there's always someone out there trying desperately to take it from them. If financial institutions are faced with this crisis, wouldn't the little merchant selling a product on the Internet be susceptible to the same risks? Does this little merchant have the resources large financial institutions have to throw against such a difficult issue?

It's not just knowing who you're doing business with on the Internet that's important, its recognizing that nobody can assure you your personal information is 100% safe.

I enjoy the benefits of on-line banking. I think it's great that I can do my banking on a computer any time I want. They already have my personal information on file anyway. Financial institutions are also monitored, regulated, policed, and have deep pockets when it comes to research, development and security issues. They have the most to lose—my trust. Without my money they don't have my business. If, for any reason my security becomes compromised at some point, I'm confident the bank I deal with will correct the error and do what they can to make me feel protected again. No promises my information will remain completely secure, but they will come to the table to protect me as we saw earlier how the banks absorbed the losses their clients experienced in the fraud scheme involving stealing client bank cards and passwords.

I don't, as a personal rule of thumb, complete any form of identification collection request on any web page, secured or not. I don't use a credit card on the Internet for any reason, and I don't fill out paper forms tipping my hand on anything that could be used to compromise my security if in the wrong hands. Now don't misunderstand, I'm not paranoid or fanatical about the subject even though I have a strong opinion, I simply have taken responsibility to protect my own identity, and have preferred to not accept on words alone when some web site tells me not to worry about my personal information being shared. Where will they be if my identity is stolen, and my credit rating destroyed?

 Home invasions are becoming more regular, and is another reason we should guard against who has our address, and knows financial information about us. Let's not give these criminals any advantage!

Let's assume we are guardians of our own personal information, and are charged with its protection. Perhaps we will think twice before offering our date of birth, social insurance number or address to just anybody who says, "I can't process your request until you give this information to me." Try saying no to them to see their response. Try walking away and finding another merchant for the product or service you're interested in before telling them more about your personal affairs. Why exactly do they need to know this information about you to sell you a product?

We live in an age were communication and security go hand in hand. Be cautious. When Spam comes through your email pitching a service that can find you your best mortgage rates, or shop your application to hundreds of lenders at the same time, or will store your personal information in a safe place, remember this; don't share anything with anybody you wouldn't want broadcasted over an Internet chat site!

Protect your personal identity
from becoming common knowledge.

Conclusion on personal borrowing

We've reviewed many ingredients to help you position your financial affairs to become sweet as spring, and right as rain. Though, at the end of the day, it takes a commitment from you to decide to take responsibility for your actions and spending behaviour to weather a storm. Put a leash on all poor spending habits now that you may have, stop impulsive shopping needs you've been satisfying. If you don't master your own wallet, you won't have much of a wallet left when you need it most.

Your credit report is your financial fingerprint, and carries a lot of weight in not only financial applications for credit, but as we learned auto insurance companies are now profiling your report to determine possible premium increases. A credit bureau report must be managed properly, and it all comes down to how you manage your financial affairs. At the end of the day the report will hold the truth about you, and you will have to sleep in whatever bed you have made.

Reading this book is only the first step. Take the time to hear the suggestions and consider the advise that has found you through these valuable pages. Now, you need to apply what you have learned to make a difference!

Good luck in your future financial affairs! I know you will now be better prepared to navigate through the labyrinth of the modern lending machine, and have confidence you will also be prepared when completing an application for credit, anywhere!

P.E.C.

What About …
Small Business Borrowers?

Look forward to reading our next book that describes how small business can prepare to borrow money from a financial institution. The overwhelming requests for this book have been heard, and we will be pleased to provide it hot off the press very soon. Look for the title *Don't Borrow Money Until You Read This Book!—Small Business*es!

Learn how to put all your ducks in a row, and understand exactly what financial institutions are looking for when considering financing for a small or medium enterprise. Why do some businesses receive more financing than others, with less security? Learn how to best present your business idea when financing for the first time. Discover the key to selling a business idea to any investor, including financial institutions! Learn how to leverage your business for start-up and for growth. You will enjoy the tour through a commercial lender's mind, and learning to speak their language to get what your business needs, when it needs it, and when it's ready to take off!

About the Author

As they are the most important in Paul Counter's life next to his faith, his wife Tracy and two children represent the strongest thread of meaning to him, and continue to mould him to be a better man, husband and father. Without them he says he would not be as encouraged or challenged to excel in helping others, a true testament to this book's grass roots.

Counter enjoys the privilege of working for one of Canada's leading financial institutions and has held various positions from investment advisor and mortgage specialist, to commercial lending for small and medium enterprises.

Seven years ago he started a small business, and has come to respect the entrepreneur more now that he has the scars to show, while saying, "I've been there and survived!" Finding a balance between family, work and business is a delicate matter of the heart. This balance is a moving bar and a difficult thing to maintain.

Owning a company has given him a better perspective on the needs of customers and clients of the bank; It-takes-one-to-know-one mentality. Understanding what it means to sweat while negotiating a new sales contract, to handling staff and banking matters for the business allows for a show of empathy for the bank's clients. He knows what it was like to not understand what the bank is looking for in a prospective client, to understanding more than they would like a customer to know!

He chooses to juggle work, family and a writing career because of their individual challenges and rewarding life experiences which enrich his character.

It is through this balancing act that Paul Counter delivers to you, a new understanding on how to get back into the driver's seat as a customer in one of the world's most needed and least understood businesses, a bank.

A Message From
The Publisher

One of the business and cultural principles that separates White Knight Publications from many others in the publishing field is our resolve to bring to our readers Canadian social issues of major concern.

When Paul E. Counter presented his manuscript to us a number of months ago, it became abundantly clear, even after reading the first chapter, that here was a book that will help many readers start to come to grips with the spending/borrowing frenzy that is all to evident in today's society. We are overly burdened with debt and shouldn't be.

The number of personal and small business bank-ruptcies increases year by year and it makes one wonder where caution has fled to and why the need to acquire, often unneeded goods and services, has become such a driving force in society. Are we totally media trained?

Borrowing money carefully, the lowest interest rates most often being available from banks and similar institutions, should be the mainstay of the mentality supporting everyone's lifestyle. Borrowing frugally and spending wisely will help us to handle debt and repayment in a way that will keep us out from under a crushing financial load.

While it is not practical to say we can all live debt free, we can as individuals stand back and take a serious look at what we are doing with the money that we'll earn today and in future. Too often bigger is NOT better, as in the case of buying a dream home on a hope and a prayer that the mortgage payments will leave a little left over for common needs.

By the time the reader, especially those starting out in new jobs or attending university, spends an hour or two on Paul Counter's information and advice, they will be a lot more in control of their future and much wiser about the use of money that will be repaying "good debt." Separate "good debt" from "bad debt" and see just where you are today and in the future.

Bill Belfontaine
Publisher

CCRA	Canada Customs and Revenue Agency
CMHC	Canadian Mortgage and Housing Corporation
FCAC	Financial Consumer Agency of Canada
GDS	Gross Debt Servicing
GROSS	Amount of income before expense deductions
KISS	Keep It Simple Stupid
NET	Amount of income after expense deductions
Notice of Assessment	Letter prepared by CCRA after reviewing an income tax return
P&I	Principal and Interest
PSOA	Personal Statement of Affairs
RRIF	Registered Retirement Income Fund
RRSP	Registered Retirement Savings Plan
Scoring Model	Sophisticated software measuring information to predict borrower trends
TDS	Total Debt Servicing

NOTES

NOTES

NOTES